TABLE OF CONTENTS

INTRODUCTION

Have you got something you never used and never bothered to throw away? Items that have started to take over a room in your house?

It is time you start to declutter your room and easily change the room \atmosphere and enjoy your house again.

Home organization can build a tidy, peaceful, and welcoming sense of being able to function effectively, and make it simple and easy to have a well-organized space. As with any venture, you must begin by knowing what you want; first thing first, you should consider the purpose of the room.

You will have to work out what you need to do, relocate, and get rid of; it may include taking everything out of the room and bring them back in an organized way. It requires a lot of effort, but with enough patience, it can be accomplished in a fantastic way.

It is crucial to understand that there are a few useful tips so that you can arrange your room to create a room that you can use and relax in. Is the purpose behind the room to watch TV, play games, study, knit, work out, sleep? Or is it possibly going to be a workplace?

Being mindful of what the space is going to be used for is necessary to create a plan and compile a list of items necessary to accomplish this task.

Assess the space to determine how much space you have and how much room you need to operate. You can even complete a quick drawing of the floor plan to see the best design possible for the space. In this way, you can drive around the furnishings with something to pick up.

You just have to take the things you have determined to hold, move, get rid of, and then do it; the ones you have chosen to discard could be thrown away, donated, or even sell out and try to make a few more bucks out of them. Go through everything and take your time to assess every object in the room. If you have left spare storage space in the room, it is perfectly acceptable to store other items less used in closets, cabinets, shelves, and cupboards. Make sure that items are visibly numbered, ordered, and appropriately arranged.

You may also opt to replace an old bulky TV or gym stuff with more modern, spatially efficient ones. It typically takes some effort to maintain a smooth and arranged space, but the benefits are worth it.

It can be extremely flattering to have a clean and efficiently organized space. Imagine your room, be bold enough to throw away the clutter, spend some time sorting, organizing and consistently keeping your room tidy. All comes down to you. If you want to do it, it can happen; you just must start.

Your home is the spot where you spend much of your time living, dining, and sleeping, with and without your loved ones; it is also the place to rest, decorate, and shed our stress to make it look perfect.

When the family is very big, this becomes a challenging job. Things like presents, dresses, magazines start to flow within the home, and it is difficult to manage and control.

Sometimes you must avoid or balance how things reach your home. You are not the only one that must learn it, the whole family must be aware of this issue. You start by listing the whole problem you are worried about; after that, create priorities based on urgency.

An example: the clothes lying around your bedroom and the excess of the dust bins in your kitchen. The priority here is to clear the dustbin because it is not only cluttered but also unsafe for your health.

Get four separate boxes, name them as: items to keep, donate, sell, and throw away. It is a smart idea to hear your favorite music to stop lurking since it is not an exciting job to do. When the house is organized, divide the collected items, and place them in the boxes you have just made.

Donate items that you no longer use, maybe children's toys, clothes, etc. Make sure they are in good condition; otherwise, you can throw it away. You should start advertising items that can be sold immediately and not keep the tasks running over the weekend.

When you organize your home, ensure that you keep the items that are most commonly used; this will allow you to locate less commonly used items, and you will know where you kept them for some time and will also be readily available. These often-used items should also be regularly washed.

Also, you must note, while arranging your house, that you should have a place for everything, and that it should only be held in that designated room.

In this GUIDE, you will discover how to organize the domestic mess once and for all and get rid of it.

Let us get started.

CHAPTER 1
HOME ORGANIZATION PLANNING

Before you start any home organization process, first, analyze your current situation and then create a decluttering plan using the following steps.

1.   Take an inventory of your home space. Put a checkmark next to each room clutter.

- Dining Space
- Living Room/Family Room
- Master Bedroom
- Children's Bedrooms
- Guest Room
- Additional Baths
- Office
- Washing machine
- Parking garage
- Other

2. Specify each room's intent. For instance, if your bedroom is for dressing and sleeping exclusively, then all the documents, photos and toys belong somewhere else. When the clothes are washed, they must be duplicated as a dungeon, the equipment, and dog food must be used elsewhere.

3. Create a list that shows the order in which each room is arranged. This allows you to concentrate on one room at a time. Tip: If you do not know where to get

started, first go for the most stressful room or location where you spend most of your time.

4. Schedule one room at a time. The one you make for yourself is your most important task. If you want to start and stick to each room and finish it, you must schedule some time for each room.

In general, it takes about 16 to 24 hours to arrange a single room thoroughly. The larger the room, the more objects it contains, the longer it takes.

Schedule time blocks that suit your lifestyle. For example, you might spend a weekend tackling a whole room, or schedule a few evenings a week for an hour or two. Do what is meaningful for you but keep your loyalty to yourself as you would to anyone else. You deserve to live in an organized environment.

1. Be sure of the why you want to organize yourself now.

What does an operational shortage cost you? Stress, missed deadlines, overlooked appointments, family disagreements?

Now relate to one of your core values, such as beauty, enjoyment, or the feeling of energy flow in your room. It will be easier to respect and accomplish your goal with an essential meaning.

2. Get the necessary resources. List all the things you need to do to accomplish this objective.

For example:

Knowledge on how to plan your tasks.

Help from family members to support you or not to interfere in this project.

Corral waste bags and gather things to be recycled.

3. Build a support network.

Who are you willing to share your progress with? Maybe he is a friend, spouse, or extended member of the family. Please ask them to keep you focused and remember your encouragement in the organizing process.

4. Define your reward

 Yeah, you are getting a reward! Whenever you go for a major target, it's important to consider the time and effort that you have spent, reserve for yourself an afternoon with friends, for a spa, or for whatever thing you think is essential and enjoyable.

5. Identify the next project.

Go back to your list, check the next objective and the schedule in your calendar.

6. Keep going! Organizing is simple but not straightforward. That said, it is worth it, and you can do it.

CHAPTER 2

IDEAS FOR EDITING YOUR HOUSE ROOMS

Imagine coming home from work to a clean and tidy kitchen, instead of clearing all the storms of the dining table. An orderly house does not have to take much time and fancy storage. Here are some tips and ideas for organizing your rooms.

General Principles:

• Begin your projects by removing everything (or as much as possible) from the space.

• Next, determine what you need in that room.

• Donate, recycle, or throw away something you do not need (a good rule of thumb is that you probably do not need it if you haven't used it in a year).

• It is always out of sight. Make sure that you do not try to fit too much in one room.

Do not forget to map your room, measure, and draw the current design with furniture.

Also draw the location of all wall sockets, light fixtures, and switches, and include doors and windows. This way, you have the critical steps with you if you need to purchase new shelves, cabinets, or other storage products.

Kitchen

Kitchens are an active environment – equipment and ingredients that are often used must be available. The kitchens often store less-used items such as pressure cookers, fondue pots, and purchases in bulk.

• After everything has been removed from the kitchen, start with the cabinets and drawers.

• Establish departments or centers of operation. Keep all your food items like flour, sugar, and starches in one cabinet together, keep canned products in another cabinet, and breakfast food in another.

• When items are placed back to your cabinets, remember where they are. Pots and pans, condiments, and spices should be next to the burner. Dishware should be near the washing machine or sink.

• Add base cabinet tray dividers to store trays, cookie sheets, muffins, and other similar articles on edge.

• Holder for pots and pans storage, placed on the wall or ceiling, is an excellent way to free up simple cabinet space. Decks can be placed in holders mounted at the back of cabinet doors.

• Pull-out baskets or shelving make it easier to reach items contained in simple cabinets.

• three-tiered step shelves make condiments, canned cans and spices, and similar articles contained in wall cabinets available.

• Consider premade islands if you do not already have an island in your kitchen. Many are on two wheels, so your room can be quickly reconfigured for your cooking needs. Your floating island can just be the place where you can hang your pans and pots.

Bathrooms

The bathrooms present some attractive storage and challenges for the organization. The environment is always warm and humid. The bathroom could be a personal one or could be shared amongst many family members or visitors.

• Consider which things you want to hide from visitors (stored behind closed doors) rather than what could be displayed (on open shelves or countertops).

• Describe the area over and above the bathroom, the toilet, the fence, the sink, or the windows of the unused space in the bathroom. Will there be a rack, a cabinet, or a bar?

If a bathroom is used by more than individual, pick cabinets that have separate areas — preferably one for every person.

Garages

Garages are the last resort storage place. They store appliances and machinery, athletic products, gardening and lawn supplies, waste, and recycling. And of course, they even store cars.

• Start by categorizing everything. This will help you identify what you need when starting a project, and at the end of a project, it is easier to put things away.

• Suggest overhead storage for products that are less used. Closed and open options are available. Just remember to list what you put in your overhead storage since it is always hard to search in them.

• If you have children, make sure that harmful and hazardous things are kept beyond their reach and in locked cabinets, if possible.

• Slat walls (as you can see in many clothing stores) are a perfect way to create the garage storage center indefinitely reconfigurable. You can place any hanger or shelf on a slat wall.

Cascading Hangers

Human beings have been hanging up clothes for thousands of years. So, it is shocking to learn that Thomas Jefferson first invented the modern clothing hanger, formed as inclining broad shoulders only to begin to fill the sleeves. Still, this first hanger was not built until the late 19th century. Even more unexpectedly, many modern clothes hanger innovations did not come until later in the 20th century.

The cascade hanger was probably the most drastic of these developments. In the center of this hanger, a hook is hanged on a line, but the sloping metal, or wood, or plastic, which fits in the robes, is duplicated, one below the other, each of which is fastened to the hanger immediately above it, instead of the holding line. Thus, a hook hanging in the closet will carry up to a dozen garments!

The waterfall hanger has different models. Some have all the attached hangers far below one another, so that the many clothing components cover a wide vertical gap. This design takes a lot of room from the clothes rod in the hold to the floor, but it has the advantage of not pressing each clothes to the other; in this way, they are more space efficient.

Not only coats or clothes use cascading hangers. Their spatial design is suitable for keeping kitchen products, plants, tools, or shelves, and can be made of wire, steel, chain, or wood.

These hangars are suitable for cupboards, kitchens, and workshops. Only recently cascading hangers have become commonly used, since their importance for the home organizer is well known through television and print.

CHAPTER 3
ORGANIZE YOUR CLOSETS WITH A CLOSET ORGANIZER SYSTEM

Cleaning a whole house can seem like an awful work, as that's how many people feel about their closets! In many homes, the closet is the most embarrassing area, but it is not too hard to organize a closet and can typically be finished in less than one day. The way to start such a project is just to clear the wardrobe.

Drop it all down to the bare walls!

If your wardrobe looks like the armchairs in my house with a door and a wooden frame, go to your nearest home store and invest in a cable rack. These systems help organize your closet to store more and yet have easy access to it, and only have a few basic hand tools easy to mount. Closet Maid makes one, but there are other closet device manufacturers.

The problem with most closets is that people, over time prefer, to throw things in without an organization, and then, things get lost! If all is arranged, you can see what you have and quickly find it. I think there are things in your wardrobe that you do not need any more or you did not even know you had. This is what always happens when I clean my wardrobe.

I notice a prolonged lack of baseball mitt or ice skates I have not seen in years!

Most people can manage the installation of a closet organizer even if you are not that handy. You will need some standard equipment such as a drill or a screw gun, a tape measure, a height, and a hammer. That is it.

To get started, calculate the size of your closet, and take it with you to the home improvement shop. Because of their low cost, the number of accessories available, most people prefer the wire shelving system for easy installation.

However, there are wardrobes systems made from other materials that are more costly but can add a finished tailored look; you can employ a specialist for a full-blown custom closet who builds you an entire storage system, but plan to pay thousands of dollars for this service. It is like a custom kitchen within a wardrobe!

I installed metal shelving systems in my house in many closets, and they are all fantastic. They helped organize the closet and expanded the available space inside, and I could execute the task in less than a weekend.

One thing most people forget is that even secret areas like drawers and closets still must have a specific organizational degree. Once people know how easy it is to have it all in the right place, they don't feel like they need to organize their closets accordingly, but the reality is that your wardrobe is as critical as making your living room space.

Clothes, shoes, sacks, bags, and other clothing materials and accessories are items that you can store in your wardrobe. If you do not arrange them, you can only spend long hours strolling through stacks of clothes to get ready to leave your home. So, to stop this, it will undoubtedly be useful to add an organizational pattern to your wardrobe. If you want to start organizing your closet today, you can follow few simple tips.

Start with a particular category. If you want your clothing to be sorted by color or by clothing type, make sure your categories are clear. For example, it would become more comfortable for you to arrange clothes based on the type of clothing articles, which shirt would fit a specific shirt, or which shoes would look great with a particular bag. Putting them in their respective categories will allow you to easily fund them when you need them.

The organization of your closet can also be done by color. You should sort the pastels out of the earth-tone colors so that you can balance them. You should stop mixing wrong colors to not look dumb anymore when you dress up.

Another way you might try is to organize your clothes according to the type of occasions they are most suitable for. On one hand, you can put your wedding robes, suits on the other hand, and casual clothes on the other. This makes it easier for you to dress up for such occasions since it is placed where it belongs.

If your closet is correctly organized, you can find your things more easily when needed. If it is kept safe and clean, it will also avoid harming your clothes due to improper handling and usage.

If you want to keep your clothes in good condition, this is a smart way to stop getting quickly worn out. You can also quickly find things that are too old or too torn to use again. This will keep you from being humiliated in public when you wear clothing that has runs or holes on it. With a well-organized wardrobe, you will be confident to look your best all the time, without having to worry about out-of-fashion or skimpy clothes.

CHAPTER 4
HOW TO ORGANIZE YOUR CHILD'S DRESS UP CLOTHES

You have children's clothes spread all over the house, from your bedrooms to the playroom, to dress shoes in the kitchen to go any time you turn around!

With three kids, two young girls and a boy with a vibrant imagination and a lot of pretenses, I will have a Sleeping Beauty Dress on my bed every day, a princess walled on the bathroom floor, dress-ups spread all over the hallway, and a pirate cape on my baby's crib. There is a massive need for some toy stores and a spot to put on the dress in our home.

First and foremost, my children are weak at hanging up things. You cannot put a dress on a hanger and to linger. Hanging it in a wardrobe is not a choice for my children.

Hooks are a suitable substitute. You can have the form of adhesive on the wall, or you can have decorative hooks on it. Your children can easily hang their princess or pirate's clothes on the hooks so to keep the floor clean and make the costumes last longer.

Another suggestion would be to buy a toybox or dress up trunk for your clothing only. Toyboxes or trunks are perfect: they are cheap, comfortable for your kid to clean up, you can place them anywhere, and they look lovely.

However, the downwards of dress-up trunks is that if they are deep, then the things on the bottom cannot be reached and so anything must be dumped out to reach them.

A plastic storage box under the bed seems to fit very well for dressing costumes. When you are about to play dress, you can get your box out and then put it back when you are done. This approach works well if toys are solely kept in the child's bedroom.

We have big built-in storage drawers for playground toys in our basement; it works great. The children should fold their clothes and place them in the large drawer when they clean. It is quick and convenient for them.

They put in the drawers their princess shoes, their capes and previous Halloween costumes. Over the years, we had to extend into many cloakrooms for their clothing, as they still ask for and play everyday clothes that seem timeless and ageless.

Clothes can be enjoyable and satisfying to arrange for you. A few minutes will make a massive difference in the long run!

CHAPTER 5
SHOE ORGANIZER IDEAS

ome people are so organized as they can put things in the right order. They allocate special places for everything they have- keys, types, books, and everything else. These are the ones who find what they need at the fingertips in the house.

On the other side, some people do not care if they bring things in. They say they easily remember where they placed things, but that does not provide a 100% guarantee. However, any time they get lost inside the fridge, they will not necessarily find their car keys.

That is why some people are well paid for coordinating things in their business. These people are the managers. Handling things well is to arrange things. Of course, running a company is not just about arranging things. In an office setting, the manager usually employs a secretary to help him coordinate his job.

If you need help to organize your home, you can hire a secretary, but this is not how things work. We receive professional advice. We read books, and we are searching for answers about how things are organized at home.

One of the hardest parts of the house is to find a place for your shoes. This is where the organizer of the shoe joins. It allows you to organize your shoes in a way that each time you need them, you can find the right pair.

The shoe organizer prevents you from using the wrong shoes unintentionally when you go to the workplace. Often catching the rush hour will sometimes lead you to trouble. You put on your clothes, brush your hair, and make sure that everything looks fine, but when you come to your office, you will notice that your shoes are black and brown.

There are several kinds of storage for your shoes-racks where you can put your shoes in pairs, the bed's organizer underneath where your shoes are placed in a perfect setting under a bed, and organizers who can put your shoes behind the door. Any of these will work well, depending on your home as well as the kind of room you have.

Nobody wants to keep their shoes in the pile of a wardrobe or the front door; however, plenty of us do! Here are five great ideas for the shoe organizer that will remove uncertainty, arrange your shoes, and finally find some budget.

1. Over-door organizers- These are popular for people who must order their shoes at a low cost. These are available in many different products, plastic, linen, or cotton. They may also be a plastic and tissue hybrid.

These typically have shoe pockets, 2 to 6 sides, which can accommodate 1 to 3 pairs of shoes per row. More than three pairs of shoes per row for the organizer pocketing and fitting on a door are quite difficult.

There are also organizers of rack-style door shoes which allow more shoes to be stored because the pocket space itself is removed.

Any considerations concerning these storage parts are whether a door is placed on the back of the door when it is opened. If there is, it might be difficult to open the door.

2. Shoe Racks- These are simple designs, it could be an armchair on the ground, or anywhere you want to hold your shoes. There can be up to 8 or more from 1 shelf. Those that buy a simple metal or plastic design can expect to pay less than a wooden rack.

3. Cubby shoe organizer-These pieces of organizers allow the consumer to store their shoes in a cubby hole. Several people do this within the front doors or other entrances, where people take their shoes off as they reach the house. These may be wood or metal framed with cubic lines.

4. Under Bed Shoe Storage- Another location where many people store shoes is under a bed. This is an excellent idea since space is usually unused. An under-bed organizer is a great opportunity for the user to position the shoes in the right arrangement. These are mostly low-level designs so that they match, and they come with handles so that the user can pull them inside as well as out of bed.

When looking at a pile of shoes and thinking about what to do about it, there are some great ideas for shoe organizers. For all sorts of budgets, there are several fantastic solutions.

CHAPTER 6

ORGANIZE YOUR HOME IN 15 MINUTES A DAY IN TWO WEEKS OR EVEN LESS

Thursday's has always been my dream day for the last few years.

Whenever I step through my front door to find my house perfectly clean, I am immediately upset, pleased as well as content.

Do not get me wrong now. Generally, my house is clean, but we have so much "family traffic" that it is always hard to have it look spotless unless you have someone cleaning you up every day.

We currently have at least ten people at our dinner table, and at least many teens in and out of the house every single day. With access to a cleaning lady once a week, this arrangement is necessary if a clean and lively household is to be maintained.

That is where my "Get Organized System" joins.

Follow these easy measures just 15 minutes a day to arrange your house in 20 or even fewer days. Nobody is planning to fail; we are just not planning.

1. Take a schedule on what to do in the next 14 days.

2. Write down which materials, such as boxes, containers, garbage bags you might need.

Start with the highest area of trafficking like your kitchen counter.

Much of the things on the counters are coming because we are too lazy to position it in the right place.

Examine your counters for the next 15 minutes to see if something can be put off or thrown out, such as junk mail or items you no longer use. Do not save it, just TRASH IT.

If you can free your counters, you will have a sense of satisfaction every time you walk into the kitchen.

Skip to the next day if your counters are empty.

3. The secret drawer.

We all have them, and most of them are loaded with garbage we did not need and must throw.

Pass and drawer for the next 15 minutes, and when you are finished throwing the whole junk, organize everything carefully. Continue to the next drawer before your kitchen drawer is done. This is a perfect workout for your young children. When I had three drawers, we were finished in half an hour with all of them.

4. Do not forget the wardrobe.

Your cabinets are also in need of order. It is always a good idea to retain a particular commodity on your shelves. For example, you should have separate shelves for the following:

- Canned goods
- Quinoa and Pasta
- Cereals and items for breakfast
- Spices and Oils

Bear in mind that your shelves must be in order. Place the most used items on the shelf that is most conveniently used.

5. Now is your Fridge Door time.

I love my children, too, but their inventions, notes, and telephone numbers have been plastered around the refrigerator door.

Remove them off from your refrigerator door and watch your kitchen shine. This is also an excellent time to search your freezer and discard old frozen foods, poultry, and so on. You should have everything you are going to need inside the fridge. Get rid of something that has not been used for over either two or three weeks.

6. Your medical office needs attention.

I keep my meds in the kitchen and thus relate this job to my cooking work. If your doctor's office is in your kitchen, miss the day we concentrate on the bathroom cabinets. Going through your medication takes treatment. Check every bottle's expiry date and throw away the expired ones away.

Make sure you have enough band helps, Neosporin and sunscreen on your shelf to ensure your first-aid kit is ready.

6. The washing machine room

I am not sure why, but my kids just love to shut the door and throw things into the laundry room. Your next stop would then be the laundry room. Purchase various color bins that stack each other on top and can be taken out quickly—store things in them beautifully, like detergents, rags, and soaps. Nice bins and well-packed things make your laundry room a place to enjoy.

7. Your Front Entrance.

When my kids were young, they would go through the door, throw their bags around the front entrance, and make the house look like a mess. It took me some time to figure out how to avoid it; the following approach works very well. Make your child feel special, give each family member a specific color.

Purchase Good Looking Bins by the entrance. That way, when you get back from school, it all goes into your bin.

At this point, I would recommend buying everything related to school in the same color for that child. If you find a green notebook around the kitchen table, do not ask anyone from who it is anymore. It can now return by the door to that green bin.

The best thing about these containers is that they are light, they can be picked up and removed during a dinner party or when you expect visitors.

8.   The bathroom is there. You must apply this drill in every bathroom in your house. Go through the drawers and throw away or do not use anything old and spoiled. Tossing shelves of baby wipes is still new in my cabinets.

Your cosmetic department needs your attention. Many items such as lipstick, mascara, and liquid makeup go poorly quickly and must be changed regularly to keep your skin safe.

9.   Bills, Holliday Cards, and Recollections.

Every bank has access to online banking, and it has never been easier to pay your bills and keep track of anything that happens to your finances. If you have not already done so, set up your online banking account today.

Purchase an expandable Staples filing folder with dividers for every month. Please buy another folder, and any time you receive a bill on the emails, it goes into that folder (this is where you store the paid bills, so when the tax season comes around, all the bills are properly sorted by month and can be tracked very quickly).

On the 1st and the 15th of each month, pay all bills in the bill folder and file them inside the other folder of the month. Simple enough, right?

10. Birthdays and special events

Let us face it; everybody likes to believe that it is part of our human existence! Why not build a personal system that recalls birthdays and family and friends' events?

I have a particular folder dedicated to all the system warranties in our house. In this folder is a schedule outlining annual checks, filter replacements, batteries, etc. It also has all the phone numbers of people I use to serve such as plumbing system and fix my appliances.

11. Now, you are ready for any bed in your home.

Keep in mind that access and reorganization can only take you 15 minutes a day. If it cannot be finished in 15 minutes, break it up in a couple of days. Do not go to the next room until you finish the room you first started.

Backpack / Charity / Other

I would think you have a pile of "things" that you do not know what to do with. This is the time you split these "things" into three batteries. Give yourself to charity, someone you know can use it, or just trash your pile. Package and Carry IT OUT appropriately, always remember to have MOVEMENT, clean it up, and take it.

12. Bedrooms.

It is time to clear your bedside tables and everything on top of it.

Do you read these three books simultaneously?

Do you need two lotion bottles on your bedside table?

Pick whatever might be necessary and place the rest in your fridge, a drawer in your bathroom, or hide them at your bedside tennis in the bottom shelf.

13. Closets.

Start your closet, and do not get distracted. Start with one part of the wardrobe at a time. Start with shirts, skirts, coats and so on.

Take away clothes that you have not worn in two years or more because you certainly will not wear them. If, for the last five years, you have not been able to get in, give them away, or throw them out. You will reward yourself with a new style pair if you lose weight again. You deserve it.

If you plan to have more children and want to store clothes for children, make a box with a label on it, identifying girls from 7 to 8 years of age. In that way, you do not have to go through all of them when you need to find a package.

14. Family Room.

The coffee table is not your old magazines' storage room. Leave one or two on the table and take the remainder to your car to read while your children play football or wait for an appointment. After reading a magazine, make sure you cast it off properly. It should not take longer than two weeks to complete this process but should organize your house and make you feel better.

This is also a perfect way for your kids to help you keep the house smooth. You will never have to blush again by opening a messy drawer if you follow this practice several times a year.

CHAPTER 7
ORGANIZING YOUR COOKING AREA TO HAVE A CLUTTER-FREE KITCHEN

I f your kitchen does not meet your needs, use the steps below to make it more comfortable.

Take stock of the purpose of your kitchens. Is it to cook, bake, consume as well as store food? If this is the case, transfer all objects not connected to your space in some other, more suitable room of your home (e.g., documents, instruments, magazines, etc.)

Identify the most relevant types of products in your kitchen. For instance:

Cookware - bowls, saucepans, and lids.

Bakeware – Cookie sheets, pie plates, cake plates, and muffins.

Equipment — coffee machine, toaster, food processor, bread maker, and mixer.

Tools - vegetable pelter, egg slicer, cork vent, box grater, opener manual, thermometer, cutting board, rolling pin, strainer, and sifter.

Utilities — spoons, spatulas, forks, tongs, brush pastry, whisks, and necessary equipment to barbecue.

Dinner glassware, plates, flatware-pots, cups, and silverware.

Managed objects - herbs, spices, dry products (meal, noodles, etc.), canned and bottled objects (soups, Worcestershire sauce, etc.)

Things for both refrigerator and freezer

Cookbooks

The wastebasket and cleaning supplies under the sink

Sort everything to the piles of the major categories listed in step 2 in your kitchen. Begin with all surface products and then move on to the stored objects in cabinets. You might want a big box for each category if you have an extraordinary number of things to sort so that your stacks do not mix.

Weed out every category and arrange it properly. Be determined to delete something other than the things you enjoy and use. Reduce many items and disposes of old and rarely used and discarded items by pitching, selling, or donating them to someone else. Then make sure to place the rest of the items in subclasses, i.e., when grouping the pantry items – placed together all spices and all dry products, etc.

Decide where each category should be held. Consider the size of each category, how often you access each category, and where you use each category in your kitchen. Place dinnerware near your dishwasher, and cookware next to your stove. Then double-check your plan – for each category, is there enough storage space available?

To make your kitchen as comfortable and fun as possible, buy containers, save space as well as accessories.

Many kitchens have a lack of room so that things such as the following will optimize and make your room more usable for you.

Take out cabinet organizers to keep things in common and offer easy access to objects in the back of your closet.

Expand steel shelves with double space in the shelf section.

Wall rack systems make it way easier to select the utensils you need while you cook.

Make sure you position all things in your new container and/or room and enjoy your reward. You will be able to obtain a kitchen that works day by day!

For many of us, the kitchen is the heart of our home, so it is necessary to keep it open as well as functional. The kitchen is normally the busiest room in the house, so it is also the best place to accumulate mess. Do not bite off more than the organized one you can chew.

It is a massive job, so one day, it is okay to tackle the cupboards and drawers and store the wardrobe and fridge for another guy. The best way to start is, as always, to delete everything from your site so that you can see everything and take stock of what you have.

Begin with the development of a staging area. Use your dining table, folding table, or split a sheet on the floor if necessary and start sorting items into different categories: kitchenware, cleaning supplies, storage products, etc. You could link all cabinets and drawers to avoid flooding the noisy kitchen in a portion of your house.

Pay attention to the duplicates.

When it is all out on your stage, you will know that the kitchen is not overcrowded due to lack of room, but because of the overflow! Multiples accumulate, and in case you need anything, you buy another one that you cannot find.

However, nobody needs three cookers. Do they?

Prepare on when you would need your gadgets, cupboards as well as your meals. Remove by letting go of a bulky ice cream maker or popcorn popper collect the powder five years ago on your fridge. Box the rest for your local cause, or if you are bold enough, for the next yard sale.

Make sense of what remains. Order them by size and locate the coordinating clothes in an unequal collection of plastic containers. Identify a drawer and use one of the larger containers to stop the lids from being lost.

If there is little room for your cabinet, consider moving your knives to a magnetic strip to ensure easy access as well as safety. If you need additional glassware, parts, or other products, but rarely use them, move them to your buffet or alternatively, store them in your saucepan until they are required.

Wipe every shelf until your cabinets are finished. Install recycled shelf liners to keep them slip-free and clean up next season. Use adjustable drawers and shelf expansion systems to maximize your storage room to make things easier to see so that you will not think about them behind your cabinets.

Several organizers are available at the sink (to pull clean supplies and plastic bags) and in the refrigerator (such as can stackers), to maximize your room and keep organized items week by week.

Make your kitchen real when you are about to place things back.

Are you cooking every day or just every now and then?

Are the children scattered here to do their homework?

Make sure any activity has a room for its business as a roadmap.

Go back to your logical "home" by positioning items where they should be used. Dishes should be close to the washing machine, so they are certainly easy to clear. Coffee and tea should be in the fridge with either your kettle or coffee machine. If you are a homework station on your kitchen island, make sure you have a basket or drawer near you.

Now that your drawers have been closed, you need to make sure that your surfaces are equally stubborn. One of the safest ways to shut off your kitchen is through the fridge door to remove something. The art of your child is precious but rich, so consider turning pieces every week instead of jamming them together. A piece is made even more impressive while creating a more visually peaceful atmosphere.

These ideas help you get the storage and make what you do more productive within your kitchen.

The kitchen is part of the home, which is also prone to both confusion and chaos, as there are many activities in the kitchen, so it is strictly necessary to organize your kitchens and keep them clean.

Moreover, some things can be used in the kitchen, requiring a lot of storage as well as a proper system. Here are some ideas and tips to help you organize your kitchen to make it a lot easier.

1. To encourage you to organize your kitchen and eradicate all its shame, find magazines and web tools where you can find ideas about the organization of your kitchen. We often need to see a cold, well-organized kitchen to keep us motivated

to proceed with this. This also allows you to prepare and envision your kitchen organization.

2. Only set the time to arrange your kitchen. Since the kitchen contains several items for the organization, it is also beneficial to set a specific time for this task alone. This way, you will not leave the job unfinished.Of course, in the kitchen, you cannot discard additional items because we also have extra dishes, cups, and saucers for potential use, which means that there is a lot to store and organize in this section of the house.

3. Sort products that are no longer available in the kitchen. Even though you can't throw away these extra items in the kitchen, you can get rid of things that no longer serve your purpose or things that have already been broken such as pots and pans that have no handles, containers without deckchairs, and many empty bottles. You may also want to clean your fridge from stale things.

4. Organize your kitchen items according to food types. Perhaps you would like to put all the spices and canned goods in one place. You may want to mark foods, especially those that look like one another, if you are using identical containers. It is essential to mark sugar and tea, salt and sugar, and many other products that can be easily mistaken for the other.

5. Keep the products that are most used within reach. When arranging your kitchen, it is conducive to position the pots, cups, and utensils that are often used. Place the least used items on your kitchen cabinets in the higher or challenging to reach some areas.

6. Drawer dividers will allow you to distinguish utensil classes. This will also allow you to use your kitchen storage areas efficiently, especially when it comes to small items as well as utensils. You may even show your china as part of your kitchen interior decoration but keep in mind that it cannot be appealing to your china cabinet.

One of the challenges could be when to start your kitchen organization. Often, too many things will steal your focus from making your kitchen unpleasant. Still, you can start your kitchen organization and work against unnecessary distractions by organizing a little bit every day, and every time you go to work in the kitchen.

Everyone needs a clean and tidy, well-ordered kitchen. However, most of the time, your kitchen and its configurations turn into a mess, and you end up not having a single idea of how to organize your kitchen so that it doesn't only get cleaner but safer as well.

There are plenty of helpful tips for arranging your kitchen correctly and making your job much simpler and more comfortable.

Additionally, there is a range of natural house cleaning items that can keep your kitchen safe and clean at the same time. Proper cleaning of your kitchen with its cabinets and appliances often helps to disinfect your kitchen, which is typically the first step towards the organization of your kitchen.

The kitchen organizing steps:

First, if you intend to organize your kitchen, you should get rid of all the unwanted things that you no longer need in your kitchen. You can either sell them for yard sales or donate them to charitable organizations. If items can no longer be used, you can dump them in the waste box. Get rid of fruit, spices, or medicines that have past their expiry dates.

Open all the cabinets and cupboards in your kitchen, remove all objects and replace all unused objects such as broken tools, etc., and then wash the drawers and cupboards properly with soapy water or natural House Cleaning products, such as an antique, soda, as well as lemon combination. It will not only clean but also disinfect your kitchen.

It is always a safer idea to store all the pots, pans, and utensils required to be regularly stored next to your stove and dishes next to your dining area or dishwasher. You can place them easily in racks or in silverware holders to create additional space in your kitchen.

As you organize your kitchen, be sure to keep sharp instruments like knives, etc., chemicals and spices far away from the children's reach and do not forget to keep items close at hand on a regular basis.

The bottles of spices and other items shall be placed in the cupboards and correctly labeled and arranged alphabetically. The most used things should also be held close at hand.

You should still use drawer divisors to have your kitchen well arranged. When your kitchen is correctly arranged, they not only provide a tidy and freshness of the kitchen but also make your kitchen more spacious so that you can function efficiently and freely in your kitchen.

The kitchen is an integral part of our house and must be held and coordinated every single day. It can also be described as one of our house's most used sections and needs the most cleaning. Make the list of all inventory items in the kitchen first. After listing, evaluate the situation, what you need, and which essential products are lacking.

- What things you use every day
- What things you use from time to time
- What things you are never using
- Do kitchen products have to be fixed or bought in case they cannot be fixed?
- Which items have doubles, that is, instead of storing both items, you can use just one object
- Which things are garbage you do not want; either sell or donate?

You should start arranging your kitchen once you have assessed the situation. This can become very easy if all the above points are decided. Place near your tools and equipment that you use several times a day.

You need quick access to these things since you must do many tasks in the kitchen. The kitchen utensils can be stored in any storage container and a drawer room saved for some other purposes.

The kitchen can be separated into different sections. Specify areas in which you can wash, cut, and cook. If you work systematically and plan things, accordingly, organizing your kitchen can be very straightforward.

You can also designate a small area where there is enough room for up to four people to sit as well as eat in the kitchen. Organizing your kitchen area gives you a good feeling every time you join. This makes your kitchen work quick and stress-free.

Now is the time to put things in order. This is where we bear in mind the kitchen areas and the items that are frequently used in them. Something to remember as well, make sure you bring the things that fit together. For instance, plates, spatulas, whiskers, and spoons should be placed near the stove; bowls, equipment, and lenses should be placed near the stove in the cooking area.

If it is not used too often such that children are unlikely to access them and potentially damage themselves, small devices, well-defined equipment, and cleanup chemicals must be stored in safe storage areas. Utensils and equipment scarcely ever used should be stored on top shelves.

Group canned vegetables by variety collectively, soup with a pot of soup, rice, and grains with other rice and grains, breakfast grain items with other full grain cereals breakfast, snacks with snack food and so on.

Organizing your kitchen will certainly make your life simpler as well as less stressed. Assigning a workspace for everything will help you discover what you need, saving you both time and energy. A clean and efficiently organized kitchen will make your tasks movement easier and make many kinds of food much more enjoyable to cook and share with your family.

CHAPTER 8

ORGANIZING YOUR BEDROOM FOR PEACE AND COMFORT - SAY IT WITH COLOR

When you have agreed to work in order to make your space your calm oasis, the real muscle work comes in! Another step is to SAY IT WITH COLOR to arrange your bedroom for peace as well as comfort.

When painting your place, a good rule of thumb is neutral – and neutral is in many shades. Find a hue that is perfect for you from whites to beiges and even grays and browns. Get color samples in your paint or home improvement shop. Bring them home to see what color your lighting to your current parts are best for you to preserve.

The bedrooms will be decorated with a flat wall that does not reflect light and look shiny. Once you have selected your color and know it is the one you want, go on, make friends, and start painting. A right, crisp white trim color will differentiate windows and doors.

Play any architectural features you may have in this space, including arches, fireplaces, chair rails, or fireplaces but remember to retain it neutral. This will not only support you when it is time to add; but it will be also appealing to most customers when it is time to sell your home.

Now that you have painted your bedroom a pretty, soft-neutral color (I like the taupe and chocolate browns personally, it is time to tie up the accessories to beat your wall color.

You will need beds, window treatments, and other accessories (squares, photographs). In case you need inspiration for colors, visit your home improvement store or display various websites online. Note that dark colors make a room look smaller, and light colors look larger.

When you hang curtains over your windows (to the ceiling), the room is taller. Some exquisite shabby curtains are made of muslin, sailcloth, or can be made from boards. No pricey, custom draperies are required to make the room look crisp as well as cozy!

You should use the complementary colors you have selected in a sparing way-do not use a bold, flashy, or busy bedding on your bed. Keep the spread easy and add a few pillows to it, or a look of color to the bottom of the blanket. If you have a desk or dresser, apply your chosen color to the baskets or trays. This helps you arrange things easier.

The bedroom can become a host of things you do not have to go anywhere else if you do not care. Many people use their bedrooms to conceal things they do not want to lie in the home.

It serves as an actual storage space for extra clothes which don't fit into the bed linen wardrobe, old photographs, electronic instruction booklets, extra sockets waiting for your coworkers, magazines, and catalogs, half-unpacked cases, and an endless list of items that might accumulate.

Sometimes it can feel like a daunting task to clean your room. Where do you put things you do not have to go to? For many people, this is a real issue.

Bedroom organization helps to identify the amount of garbage you have. Break them in bags of paper, boxes, washing baskets, or just break the batteries on your bed. First, start with the largest products. If you have a heap of jackets, hang them in a different bedroom or try to keep them in the wardrobe.

Shoes at the bottom of your closet should have a special place. If you store photo albums and stacks of books in your wardrobe, you need to transfer them to another room you don't use so much, whether you need to install shelves for storage in your wardrobe or invest in a cedar chest or two to keep up the chances.

Have your washing done at once and throw away all the socks that have no buddies. If you think the mates appear, hold a small basket on a closet rack for the replacement socks. Add to it and go through it roughly once a month. This lets you decide which socks you must go to.

Bills, junk mail, receipts, magazines, and catalogs are typical items to be installed on a cloakroom or desk. Take all of them and get them sorted. Keep only catalogs for places you cannot shop online.

Recycling or donation of magazines to a doctor's office or hospital hall may be necessary. If you like any of the articles, go through them and pick whatever you think it might be necessary.

Either scan them, hold a file on your computer, or tape them onto notebook paper, and start a three-ring binder with exciting or informative objects. Hold a magazine rack nearby in case you read them in bed.

Maintain the binder, scissors, and tape in the rack of the magazine. Get yourself used to cut off things you want to hold.

Create a unique billboard and invest in a shredder. Make any bill you pay a point of shredding. Organize and keep your clothes tidy with wooden hangers on your wardrobe. Place your dresser drawers as often as possible so that they do not get filled up and turn into heaps of laundry.

When your wardrobe, cloakroom, tables, desks, and chairs are uncomplicated, it is up to you to do this. Identify hot spots and solve the stacking problem.

A well-organized space is not only about finding things you want but also creating a welcoming environment where you are able to relax and work efficiently without the burden of clutter.

You must decide what you want to do with the room while arranging it. You must know what to hold and what to throw away. You can have space in the way you want it to be given a little time.

What is the purpose of the space, TV, sleeping, games, whatever the primary purpose would be?

Then list the things you want in the room. Of course, these aspects should serve the room's primary function. Then place these things in the room; they make sense.

Remove items in the room that do not serve the room's purpose. Do these things belong there, or you just must get rid of them in another room? — Next, place what you want to hold in the room strategically.

You want to take note of the items you carry and how you put them; after all, you get rid of clutter and don't lay the ground for the room to retract. Ensure the storage in the room, drawers, armoires, closets, etc. are used effectively and not as catch-calls to collect more items.

It is adorable to have your room properly planned. Make sure you throw out all the junk and arrange for the rest. Hold your newly organized space in your hands if your space is arranged.

CHAPTER 9

ORGANIZING YOUR BEDROOM FOR PEACE AND COMFORT BY DEFINING THE SPACE

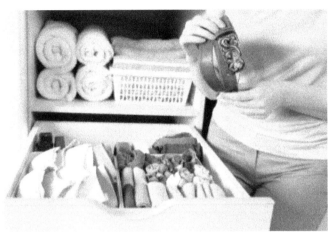

I s your bedroom a quiet as well as relaxing place?

Are you scared of wading every night in piles of clothes and an unmade bed?

There are some straightforward measures to make this space a place of calm.

The first step would be to identify space. Many do not even consider the function of a bedroom apart from the apparent sleep and romance! But you would be shocked how much this space is ignored since it usually is your home's least seen space.

In your bedroom, there is a tendency to pile up clutter-clothing, shoes, books, magazines, and work on projects. If it is from the house's key traffic areas, no one is going to see it anyway, right?

But what does this do for YOU?

A sense of anxiety and stress arises when the time comes to retire in the evening. You know this morning you didn't make your bed, that the laundry is on the chair, and that your intention is to read a pile of books on your bedside table and the list can go on and on.

The main thing is to define the space. Do not let your bedroom be a pseudo-office or a catch for anything you cannot bring through. Your bedroom can only be used as follows:

SLEEP / ROMANCE – this seems apparent but is the bedroom's most critical usage. Later, I am going to explore how harmony and prosperity can be taken to bed by using bedding and color. The rest is all yours!

STORAGE – you need to use the bedroom to store things such as clothing, shoes, cosmetics, and gemstones, but I will show you innovative, simple as well as cheap ways of doing so.

RELAXING – it is one of your bedroom's most critical things, and I will share tips on how to build that sense of calm and peace while preserving its shape and work.

Nothing more! Note that no food or job is mentioned above. You now have a good idea of what your bedroom should be like. When you start organizing this room for its function, you will start looking forward to bedding and relax in the oasis you have built!

In summary, you always start by identifying the function of your room and then by deciding the focal categories in space, sorting all items into the main categories, and finally changing each main category to what you enjoy and use.

The next step of the organizing method is to reassemble your room, and that is where the actual problem is solved. Your goal is to achieve smart, space-saving solutions, which enable you to arrange, contain as well as organize rooms and items that start with your bedrooms.

Build a restful, tidy bedroom with the following materials and ideas:

Your Wardrobe -Dress easily, conveniently, and happily.

Closet organizing package – this form of device maximizes your room and can be personalized according to your business needs. Measure the cupboard area and count the number of suits, skirts, tops, dresses, sweaters, shoes, and bags in your wardrobe before you buy this package. Go home to the finishes and parts and buy the one that best suits your needs.

Bottom shelf basket-This is a plastic wire basket, which slips on a rack for further storage.

Shelf divisor-This gadget slides over the front edge of a shelf to help stacked objects and avoid the stacks falling over. It is the perfect choice for sweaters.

Stacking shelf - a perfect solution for those areas where permanent shelving is not needed. Purchase one or more storage units and make the most of your vertical space.

Multi-pocket Device Over the entrance-A perfect place to stock shoes, bagpipes, belts, jewels, and scarves. Choose one with transparent plastic pockets and recognize the contents quickly.

Hanging linen shelves- This tool connects to your closet rod and adds a selection of sweaters, t-shirts, jeans, etc. They are also perfect for arranging different sports equipment or clothes for children on any given day of the week.

Pegs – It makes it easy to keep your bedroom clean by adding a pair of pegs or a pegboard to your wardrobe. Only slip on and off your PJ, robe, and some other things you often use.

The hamper-Each room needs a hamper washing machine. Hang a canvas bag on the rod or a hook if there is room in your closet to make it easy to throw dirty clothes on the right spot.

Lighting – Decent lighting helps ensure that you do not take a brown shoe and a black one. It encourages the assembly of an outfit as well. With Stick and Click lights, you can install lighting without cabling, which requires only three small batteries.

Stool - Consider adding a stool if you have enough locker space so you can reach upper shelves and sit on your shoes. Even better, take a stool with two duties: choose one that has storage plus chairs.

Hangers- Wooden hangers do not just look fantastic in your wardrobe-they are better able to carry your clothes. Consider the form with a ribbed bar in which pants are kept because this arrangement prevents rubbing.

Your bed – Make your bed your room's focal point and use it for storage if your space is difficult.

Location – Position your bed to allow a clear view of the door, but not putting it opposite the door or on the wall of the door.

Linen-Use the most delicate quality fabrics and coordinate them with the calming wall color.

Platform-If your room is cramped, invest in a bed with drawers, cabinets, and baskets. You can get a lot of small things in these compartments.

Risers – Another choice for your spatially challenged bedroom is the use of plastic under bed containers for shoes, linens, out-of-season clothes, and wheels. If you want this option, please use a bed skirt to keep your warehouse out of view.

Your media – Go to the room to watch TV, and then cover it when you do not want to watch it.

Deluxe options - cover your TV from your bed in a pop-up drawer. Or splurge on a personalized cabinet that rotates 180 degrees to your TV so that when you do not use it, you only see bookshelves.

Dresser-If you do not have to dig around your house for a new dresser if you purchase one of the above pieces. Place the TV above, build a box, and add doors to the front.

Your Nightstand-This object should be useful, i.e., carry an alarm clock, book, and glass of water.

Light-Instead of lighting your nightstand, look for lighting that mounts like a photo on the newer wall choices.

Popular household pieces-Your bedside tables do not need to be classic- you can use a wall fitted chair, bench, end table, small dresser, or shelf. If you want a bedside table on either side of the room, note that they do not have to be the same. It is crucial that you feel your room is relaxed as well as convenient.

CHAPTER 10

ORGANIZE SHELF SPACE IN YOUR HOUSE AND HAVE A FRUITFUL REORGANIZING BLITZ

I f you plan to spend a day decluttering your home, consider arranging a lightning shelf. Instead of fixing those rooms in your home, make sure you concentrate on places where storage is underused. Often it is the humble shelf that is overlooked when your house is reorganized. So, let us start organizing shelter space efficiently in your house.

You may live at a place that has already installed some cupboards with ample shelving space, depending on the design of your home. If that is the case, it is going to be your decluttering session. The answer looks right in front of you. You just need to reorganize your property in your home so that your shelving room can be appropriately used.

Let us peek at your house's shelving area from your bedroom closets. First, consider how you use your shelving room.

Are the racks full of all kinds of possessions?

Do you see plenty of space in your cupboards along the shelves?

Try to match the storage somewhere between them.

One of the tricks to use racks efficiently is to reorganize the items in your racks to keep the correct number of items and related items together.

Let us get started and refine the area you wanted to clean up and reorder. Let us assume that is your dormitory closet, and you wanted to tackle the dressing racks. Before you remove all your belongings, make sure you check your closet's current condition. Examine how well things are stacked and whether there is room between objects. Check out how well things fit on the racks.

Objects can be stored in either free form or storage boxes. Take notes on the present method of organization. If you have completed this exercise, you are able to better develop some brilliant ideas about how to boost your storage.

Some people find that adding additional shelves between the current ones helps to create additional storage space. Others prefer to boost their storage by buying storage boxes as well as containers to store products. Start brainstorming ideas to see if you can use your shelves better.

Now that you are brainstorming a little, it is time to clear all your belongings from the shelves. Take a clean rag and wipe the closet down. Look at your wardrobe. Take into consideration the amount of storage space that you have as well. When your belongings are gone, your closet would have more than enough room often. Let us be careful to keep it that way when you return things to the wardrobe.

For your decluttering exercise, you should have two goals.

First, aim to put less than what you took out on the shelves. Secondly, strive to boost your closet's existing room. This can include the procurement of new containers or the installation of new racks. Using an organizing flash to declutter your closets can turn out to be a completely satisfactory experience.

CHAPTER 11
ORGANIZING YOUR WARDROBE

P eople clean their houses every year in the spring. Surfaces are scrubbed, ovens washed, and a clean makeover is provided to the garage, but generally, what do we fail to clean? OUR WARDROBES

It can be a bit discouraging to organize your wardrobe, especially if you do not know where to start. However, what is important to note is that organizing your wardrobe will help you to optimize what is already there. Quite often you might even find that you do not have to buy new clothes because there is plenty to last for about a year.

It is highly advised to begin organizing your wardrobe with pants management. It may seem tedious, but every pair must be tried to ensure it is still in place. Do not make lame excuses, as you would wish it would finally suit you after your diet. Karma laws forbid misunderstanding.

Furthermore, your common sense of fashion should tell you that you need clothes in the right size to look good. Separate your summer pants from your winter pants. When the seasons shift, finding the right pants is easy.

It is much harder to arrange your tops. You must arrange them according to the season. You should be distinguished from what you wear in summer or spring during winter. You must distinguish what you wear at work during the day and at parties or night outs during the evening. You do not need too much space for this.

Like any other thing in your wardrobe, they should be appropriately stored and divided into seasons. There is no point in handing out your winter clothes so that you can make space for your summer dresses and be sure to store them correctly to prevent permanent plugging.

Sort and stock

If you are not out and do not need your cocktail dresses, store it to make room for your regular clothes.

Each pair should have a rail or box of its own. Many women enjoy shoes and are generally more interested in showing them. Shoes last longer if you take appropriate care and do not stack them at the bottom of your wardrobe.

Your jewelry and accessories should be color-coordinated for quick selection. Scarves, belts, gloves, and hats require a separate section from your earrings, collars, wristbands, rings, and shovels. It would be great if you had many pairs of cufflinks or earrings if you had a great cushioned box to hold the pairs together.

This can save you a lot of time, incredibly, if you are rushing to a meeting.

Get rid of the clothes you do not intend to wear, so you have enough space for new, more trendy pieces. Try it all to make sure it all suits you. You cannot expect that your body was the way it was ten years ago. The clothes that suit you then, most likely, will not fit you the same way. Be bold enough to embrace improvement. Organize your wardrobe today.

Most people go to the living room when they want to get a house cleaned. After all, when people visit, that's what people see, and nobody wants their friends to think their home is cluttered; however, there are two good reasons why the bedroom is one of the best places to start a decluttering job.

(1) You spend more time in a room than in every other room in the House, and (2) Good night's sleep is more comfortable if your room is a restful sanctuary from the clutter that occupies the rest of your house.

Fencing

You need to have space to place them before you can "clean up and put things away," Take a look at the cabinets in your bedroom. Consider the wardrobe first.

Are your clothes so tightly packed together that you cannot even see what is there?

Much worse, are they so entangled that you cannot even wear them when you can pull them out?

If so, this is a good starting point for your company.

Take everything, one object at a time, out of the wardrobe. You may put items in stacks on the bunk, whether tops, dresses, blouses, or something. You may want to distinguish your clothes from where you wear them: working, bathing, around the house, etc. Before you pile it on your bed, look at every single object.

If you know that it does not suit you and will never wear it again, put it in a separate stack or send it to a friend. If you just do not like it again, well, you do not want to give it to a friend or a thrift shop, just place it in a different pile.

Until the closet is empty, wash the walls for a few minutes. When everything is pushed out, this job becomes much simpler! Consider purchasing such cabinet organizers; they will allow a lot more storage space. Maybe you can hang another rod in the ground halfway.

You have now doubled the shirts and blouses room! In the meantime, just grab the batteries and put things in groups in the closet – and everything is organized! Bet, you are going to spend much less time trying to find what you want to wear.

Dressers

The next move is to look at your cloakrooms. After all, there are plenty of garments to place in drawers rather than hangers. Follow the same process: remove items from one drawer and position them in suitable stacks. Do not forget the shop pile of the friend/thrift! The more things you get rid of, the less room you need to find.

This is the time where you look at potential alternate storage areas. What about your bed underneath? There is plenty of room underneath, especially if you have a queen or king-size bed. You should slide storage containers out of the way under the bunk. This is particularly useful for saving things from season.

Perhaps you might place an enticing trunk in the bed's food. It contains many things, perhaps those bulky blankets or additional pillows. You would have the bonus of sitting and tying your shoes in the morning.

All right, for now, that is enough work. You solved your closet, which was the biggest challenge in your space. If you have tamed the beast, you can go further in other ways to degrade your bedroom, but that's another day's tale (task and a).

Ways to Organize Your Wardrobe for Better Housekeeping Services

1. Organize according to the season. Store clothes in plastic bins according to each season. Keep in your closet one or two emergency robes but, otherwise, keep a lean

as well as functional wardrobe—Mark each bin so that you can quickly and easily decide the material.

2. Sort by color.

3. In your wardrobe, sort by color from black to white. This will allow you to identify every object you are looking for by having a color-coded organization. In case you have many things of one color, hold them nearest the closet door.

4. Fold carefully. Crumpled shirts and rolled jeans take up more room than pliable objects but by keeping your plugs close and your plugs small, you can optimize your shop space so that more tools and supplies can be preserved.

5. Place your most used things near the handle of the closet door. Sort often first by color but remember the rule of thumb (or rather arm length): things from the closet door that are easier to grab are the ones that you wear most of the time. Store small used straps and boots in the far corner, leaving your slippers and purses near the wardrobe entrance.

6. Donate and discard old things periodically.

7. Do not let the closet stagnate. Sort your things once a month (or at least twice a year) and make a pile of charity. If you find things that have been worn or torn, make sure to throw them away. This cut keeps the closet new as well as ready for more purchases during the season. Treat the goodwill with a new mall outfit after the donation is dropped.

8. Push each item to wear once before you can reuse another item. Do you have you more blouses than you could count? Before you can wear another previous item, wear each item once. This lets you discard neglected old appliances that would sneak through the gaps of your wardrobe otherwise.

9. Hang laundry the same way.

A nice closet is a happy wardrobe, and a happy wardrobe makes you proud to be clean and organized—Orient your hangers to your shirts and pants hanging in the same direction. Make sure there is enough space for your belongings; wrinkling can happen if you are restricted to a small area.

10. Encourage the whole household to do the same.

There is strength in numbers, and it would be easier to keep the routine up if the whole family supports the efforts. Set a timetable for contributions and periodically reward the efforts of the whole family. After several months, without realizing it, you will begin to plan.

11. Keep your linen with scented refresher items. Nobody likes to smell like mothballs or mouthpieces. It is highly recommended to hang car air fresheners in your wardrobe or placed jackets on a stand. When you use them, your clothes will stay fresh, and there is no need to spend a fortune on extra dry cleaning between uses.

12. Set limits for yourself. Do not let your laundry go unsorted for more than a day. By setting boundaries, you are pushed into a healthy as well as optimistic routine. Follow the boundaries and enjoy the glory of a safe and tidy living area.

By following these quick tips, your overflowing cupboards and drawers are tamed in no time.

CHAPTER 12

SIMPLE STEPS TO ORGANIZE AND LIGHTEN YOUR LOAD

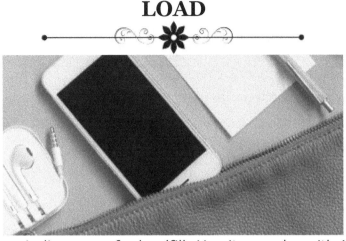

I s your bag reminding you of a landfill. Has it gone by with journals, make-up, and odds-n-ends? Does your weight dig into your shoulder? If so, do not let the sun go, detach the contents, and organize your things so that you can easily find what you need whenever you want it. Here is the way:

Remove the clutter. Empty your bag material on a flat surface. Then, follow the next steps:

Pitch all wrappers, fabrics as well as papers.

File receipts for tax or assurance purposes and shred the rest.

Make up the critical elements for quick touch-ups. The same applies to other individual objects.

Reduce drugs to one day's supply.

Go through your wallet and throw everything away except the simple ID and a few credit cards. Reduce cash and bank balance to a minimum. Pick a checkbook and put the others away if you need to bring one.

In a picture box or album, position, loose images.

Send excess supplies to your home office (stamps, envelopes, pens, etc.).

Remove both books as well as magazines.

Give or wash all clothes in the wardrobe.

Bunch of technology products, i.e., your phone, your PDA, etc.

Gather all the goodies you wore to entertain and set aside your son/daughter.

Contents Comparison

Group items like and keep each group in a small case, bag, or pouch. For example, you can only carry three cases in your bag: one with cosmetics, one with personal items, and one with financial items. Use tiny, easily distinguishable instances; you can easily record what you desire in seconds. Certain options are:

Cotton Zip packs. Check out Walker bags in plenty of appealing colors for noticeable case textiles.

Zip Lock Bags. Clear plastic bags let you see what is inside; they are budget-friendly and available in foodstuffs and pharmacies.

A Purseket. This is a removable panel of lightweight bags, available on Purseket.com.

Arrange your things. If you have a handbag with lots of pockets or a tote without compartments, it is easy to organize your bag contents when you follow these suggestions:

Purse with boxes

Think of the arrangement of your bag as if it had three circles: 1st, open interior, 2nd inner pocket, and 3rd outer pocket. Place large valuables (wallet, phone, PDA) in the inside of your pocket.

Place smaller medium-value objects in separate interior pockets (keys, prescription, cosmetic products). Use the external pocket to capture receipts as well as notes all day long. When you come home at night, take away all the papers and process them accordingly. Set your bag always this way, and you can never waste time searching again or anything else for your keys.

Purse or tote without bags. Hold things in individually colored cases together and avoid the cases. Placed left the most valuable cases, the medium value articles in the middle and right side of the tote the least valuable cases.

Tips and additional notes:

Bring a different children's tote, sweets, etc. In this way, you will not have to lug anything, including your own in both kids while making shortstops in the supermarket or dry cleaners.

Whatever you get the chance to, wear the smallest handbag-it sets a default limit on what you can carry around.

Choose a comfortable, short, large straps shoulder bag. Short straps hold your bag's weight tucked under your arm, where managing is easier and on the back safer.

Purses are prey to shame, and when you are away from home, they are the only place to stash items. Make it a habit to empty your bag every evening, particularly your external pocket. That way, you will not bring more than you need or forget to look at memorabilia for the next day.

As an additional bonus, each time you open your pack, you are greeted with a much tidier look.

CHAPTER 13

DECLUTTER YOUR HOUSE AND KEEP IT ORGANIZED

I t's four season times a year. The seasons are changing, and our habits are changing with them. Spring cleaning, fall cleaning, shopping, recreation, yard sales, summer

holidays, winter holidays, dog care. There is an infinite list of new beginnings as well as new organizational prospects.

You may have agreed to do it with fun next season, but how do you do it all? First, I believe in the importance of a homeless home.

It is much easier to keep the house tidy. You can quickly dust, mop, and vacuum when stacks of things are not to pick up. The removal of belongings is often easier.

It looks and sounds so beautiful! Whether for your enjoyment or the pleasure of knowing that you are prepared for something, it is nice to live in a sleek as well as beautiful environment. It is all in its place. You can also decorate, if you like, or take this hobby for which you have never had time before.

But it is a busy season every season. When you have no time, how do you declutter?

Answer: do something every day. That is the key.

Do not write off a day because you cannot spend hours on the job. Today, you should do anything. Five minutes spent daily will do a great deal. Fifteen minutes will move mountains every day!

Next, locate the magnetically cluttering area of either your house or apartment. It could be a specific table, a kitchen counter, even a sink! Make it your # 1 project, whatever it is.

Just do not clear the drain, let it shine!

Let us say your dining table is the hot spot. Review the situation. Look at what is there overall. You can say to most, "this doesn't belong here."

You are using an empty basket or box for washing. Put in a basket everything that belongs to the same area of the house, including the bedroom. Go to the place where the products are. If you have some time, put it away, but do not be fascinated by it. You are on a timetable.

Decluttering the table would be your main goal. Mainly if the ECO is an emergency clean-up operation, leave it in a nice pile to care for each owner. (Possibly a nice note on top of the pile is required to let your family know why it is there.

Go straight back to the table in the dining room. Do not get sidetracked.

Are you aware that most of us allowed clutter to ascend because we are perfectionists?

The role seems intimidating at first sight because we want it to be okay. Only the visual of something to do will avoid a perfectionist right on her (or his) roads! The first thing to do is to accept that it will NOT be flawless. This is a small strategic assault on a significant issue that you can solve over time.

So, come back to the ASAP table. Take the next group of things and take them to their location. You should now be able to finally see the table surface! Make a fast dusting and make it look pretty!

Finally, place a lovely centerpiece or vase with flowers in the middle of the table. That tells you and the rest of your family that the table is now clutter-free! It looks too good to get rid of it! This technique works fantastically!

Nobody wants to be the first person to bring their things in there, so it will stay clean for a while. Make up your mind that you are not going to let it go the way it was. If you leave something not on the table, someone else will do the same.

This whole project can be completed in about 10-20 minutes, not a day. Only stand back and look. It looks good, isn't it? Isn't that feeling good? Tomorrow, you will move on to the next decluttering point. Do a little bit each day, and your home will soon be tidy, organized, and beautiful-ready for everything!

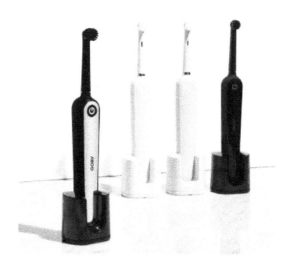

CHAPTER 14

DIY WAYS TO ORGANIZE & UPDATE YOUR BATH

E mpty the room first and edit all your things. You must sort things out and let go of duplicates, items that nobody uses, expired medications as well as make-up. You need to remove everything except the things you are going to use.

Give it a facelift before you cart all the things you need to hold back in your room. You can create a safe, practical, and vibrant bathroom, smart storage, and simple surfaces to clean. Start at the top and work all the way down to the field.

Ceiling-Don't skip it over even though you do not spend a lot of time staring at your ceiling.

Paint – If you have been painting the room for some time now, refresh it with a new coat of no-VOC ceiling paint and if you have any winds in the roof that look dingy, take it out, wash and spray low-VOC.

Ventilation-A fan prevents smells and humidity that can contribute to mold in the bathroom. With, make sure your fan works properly. Take off the cover, wipe it off, and spray low VOC (volatile organic compound) paint on the cover whenever necessary.

Walls — One of the most drastic and inexpensive improvements you can make in your room is to refresh the walls.

Fix – Add a packaging paste to create a smooth painting surface if you have nicks or tiny holes in your wall.

Paint - Pick a color for your walls to convey your unique style. However, it is a good idea to avoid a dark color since it could distort reflection in the mirror that could lead you to make-up too much. The type of paint to be used is another significant factor. Choose a semi-gloss for the kitchen and paint the bathroom.

This paint is easy to scrub and is resistant to mildew. Finally, there are several color options available for low or no VOCs.

Cabinets – Every bath requires underground storage. Measure the number of materials you want to hide, measure your usable room, and then buy a device that suits your style and budget.

Vanity – A real plus is a spacious vanity. You can ruin the toiletries of any family member in a convenient organizer, store clean towels, and no one will be wiser. Turning an antique dresser into a vanity is a smart way of going green. If you do not have a new vanity in the cards, splash a fresh paint coat on your current vanity and install new hardware to get a new look.

Cabinets are the best place to store unexpired drugs and medical goods for treatments such as headaches, wounds, burns, coughs, colds and so on. Not only are modern medical offices functional, but they are also wall art.

They are available in a different range of types and forms and can also be obtained with fog-proof mirrors. If the current medicine cabinet has a wooden or laminated cover, update it with the same calming color you use on the walls.

Water Hogging Devices – Nearly 60% of the consumption of indoor domestic water is in the bathroom. Here are a few things you can do to avoid and save some dollars on your consumption.

Shower Head - Upgrade the showerhead from $10.00 to $50.00 to a low-flow model. This move decreases the amount of water you use without interfering with results.

Smart tip: A bath uses more water than a quick shower.

Faucet - Get a low-flow faucet aerator, easy to mount, and available for $3.00 to $10.00. The system combines air with water to minimize water consumption. Look for a rated 2.75 GPM or less (gallons per minute).

Flooring-Patch it now in case the floor of your bathroom has streaks, tears, or worn vinyl.

Linoleum-Linoleum is one of the most durable, affordable as well as environmentally friendly flooring choices. It is primarily made of linens oil and is available in hundreds of colors. Even though both tiles and sheets are available, stay with linoleum sheets as the tiles can appear in the corners.

Vinyl-Some of the latest peel and stick vinyl is a cost-effective way to refresh your floor look. You can quickly mount it yourself and save on labor costs. Besides, some existing materials may be placed. This product is available in 12 and 18-inch squares so that colors and patterns can be easily combined. Clean-up is a breeze; wash it off with either a wet cloth or mop.

Tile-This product is lovely, robust, and simple to look after. If you plan to buy it, make sure you pick a moisture-resistant as well as slip-resistant tile. The installation differs from simple to demanding, which is why you need to decide.

Organizers and accessories-it will be easier to keep your bathroom tidy, secretive, and organized if you use any of the devices mentioned below:

Wall hooks one for each family member so that after showering, they can hang their dress or damp towels, and small children are able to use this method without assistance.

Shelving-Go vertical and add wall shelves when the cabinet storage does not suffice. Reuse old lumber in the garage, if necessary. Then buy a basket, mark it with your name and add to your toiletries for everyone.

Over the door, hook rack-This convenient organizer has up to 6 hooks. Just slide it over the door; the door closure will not interfere. This system catches any kind of clothes quickly.

Pocket Shower Curtain-Double duty of this smart gadget. It is a shower curtain, and it includes storage pockets. The shower curtain may be used as a cabinet or as a stand-alone curtain, with pockets facing inside or out of the shower.

This item is perfect for easy storage of beauty items and bath toys.

Intelligent tip: If you intend to buy a decorative shower curtain, search for one made of hemp because it avoids mildew.

Adjustable bucket for your shower-This makes a smart unit that sits on your head and has two shelves going up and downside by the side to accommodate big bottles. This caddy contains many items, plus bottles can be kept upside down to make distribution easier.

CHAPTER 15

ORGANIZING YOUR FAMILY ROOM

I s the meeting area (a.k.a. family space), dining room messy as well as unkept in your home? If this is the case, aim to build a peaceful, comfortable, and tidy space to relax in and entertain both friends and family.

Make sure you pin down your room's purpose(s). Is it your plan to watch movies, curl up and read, play with the girls, take a quick nap, and meet friends in the family room? If you think about the above functions or something else, you should move items not related to your room's purpose (shoes, clothing, and the ironing board) to a separate as well as more suitable location.

Specify the key categories of things in your family room. For example:

Reading – books, magazines, and journals

TV, VCR, DVD, stereo, recording, CD, DVD, and remote media

Toys-pounds, figures for action, and vehicles

Games – board games and cards puzzles

Collections-videos, paraphernalia baseball, etc.

Sort everything out into piles in your family room that reflect the key categories listed above. Start with all surface items and shift into artifacts contained in baskets, cabinets, and drawers as well.

Smart tip: If you have not edited your items for several years, you will definitely find it easier to organize a large number of items by using a large box containing each major category; the boxes ensure that your piles do not scatter and thus get mixed up.

Cut off the mess and sort whatever is left. Evaluate each object with a single category at a time by following rules: do not hold something you enjoy or use, minimize multiples from one object, recycle everything but the latest version for magazines or newspapers; dispose of damaged and discarded objects by pitching them, selling or giving to somebody else. Then arrange the rest of the products.

Remove, for instance: duplicate images, out-of-focus images as well as unflattering photos. Then organize your pictures by date or subject, such as home, family, school, holidays and so on.

Smart tip: When you eliminate clutters from each essential category, leave 20% more things to go than you have room for, new acquisitions will have their homes ready.

Make your room comfortable and usable as well. If you have a room that serves some purposes, make sure you consider setting up your room in zones-each for another operation.

For example:

Reading and playing sports: Place a play table and chairs where you have good light; it is a perfect place to play paper and the board games. The same top of the table can also be doubled as snacks if you have mates. Build a bookcase on the adjacent wall with books as well as gaming materials.

Pick a suitable place to hide electronic devices in your cabinet if you do not want to see it. Coordinate the layout of the main seating elements so that you can conveniently view the screen (and use the view where considered necessary). Place a magazine rack next to it and throw a plump sleeve over it so that when relaxing, you can cover up and catch a catnap.

Playing

Stick toys in baskets or storage ottomans that merge with the areas mentioned earlier on. These containers are a perfect way to store disruptive chaos and turn the family room into an open space for adults after the children have fallen out into the dreamland.

If required, use containers around your home to access and contain easily accessible objects. Family rooms are a magnet with books, journals, and supplies stacked up on the floor and the tops of the table. However, these things can be arranged with budget friendly solutions that you most likely have around your house.

The same size and color shoe boxes can be used for videos, notes, CDs, and more. Use many containers of the same color, and symmetry lifts the ordinary to an elegant set.

It can be used for books, magazines and newspapers, fruit crates, baskets, and durable totes.

Pottery, glass jars, and bowls hold fine for styles, clips, bands of rubber, and push pins.

Ice cube trays, muffins, box lids, and cup trays make perfect drawer organizers.

Vintage baggage and picnic baskets are stacked on top of one another and work alongside tables to make storage sturdy and attractive.

Slip things into their new ship and place them where they are beautiful as well as functional. That is, it! You now have a family room that is easy to clean, and that uses your space intelligently.

CHAPTER 16
ORGANIZE YOUR LAUNDRY

Sort out weekdays, weekends, or evenings, instead of making your washing feel like an endless task, which would be easy to do and try to get into a routine.

Do not wash clothes only because they were once worn. It is not only a waste of our most important resource – water – but a waste of your time as well. If it is not filthy, bring it back and wait until it is filthy. Isn't it a no brainer!? So, you have no reason to wash unless you have Obsessive-Compulsive Disorder (OCD).

Start Young

In case you have children, get them in the habit of placing their dirty clothes into the laundry basket as required and take them away when they are dry. When you have different rooms, use multiple baskets-one for lights, another dark, towels, and sheets that are marked for children to learn.

It is a fantastic idea to have a laundry chute in your design in case your house is on two floors. I know it is enough to be green with envy if you do not match the category but try to be grateful for your happiness!

Shop Wisely

Washing detergents etc. are big times, so make sure you keep an eye on good specials and buy them big. This only applies to those who have enough space to properly store it. Otherwise, it could save you money but not your health when your house is filled with items that were unique to you, but you unfortunately do not have space for it. Note Balance for everything-including a great deal!

Using your shopping list

I still want to have two laundry detergent packets in the cupboard. So, if you have to buy one or two more packets, you will never get caught paying more-especially in our local supermarket, definitely not one where you want to pay the full price in any situation unnecessarily!

Take note of the environment

Make sure you buy eco-friendly detergents and pre-things removers. It changes the world, and the price is comparable to the nasties out there now, so there is no reason!

Mending

Have a clothes position that needs to be patched and remove the needle and the thread during the advertisements of your favorite TV show.

Similar odds and ends

Keep items you find in the laundry, such as money and buttons, in a small jar.

Think smartly

With the clothing/fiber technologies, you are not expected to buy 'Dry-Clean Only' clothing these nowadays.

Save yourself, the world, and your hip pocket and stop it all. The exact same thing goes for clothes that need to be ironed when you wear them and then let them wash. Dream of what you can do with all the time saved!

Organizing your laundry helps you to build space and time for you as well as your loved ones. This provides you with the resources to manage yourself, family, house, work, and finance in your daily routine.

CHAPTER 17

HOW ORGANIZING YOUR GARAGE IMPROVES EFFICIENCY AND REDUCES FRUSTRATION WHEN COMPLETING TASKS

Garages tend to be one of our homes' most disorganized areas. For most people, the organization of their garage is seen as a colossal challenge, so we doggedly avoid this location.

If we want to be as efficient as possible, an organized garage is essential. An organized garage means that everything can be placed so that tasks can be done quickly, if necessary.

Garages get messy since we like to stack items in corners, stack them on a wall or place them on a flat field. Our garage is full of things that we do not need or want shortly, and we are not able to figure out what we want when we need them. Searching for software or other equipment frequently decreases productivity and induces frustration when trying to complete tasks.

Does your garage double as a warehouse? Is this the place where you can find your overflowing containers of old, unlabeled pieces, beach accessory, and Halloween customs?

Do you have problems finding your gardening equipment whenever you need it?

Are all your tools distributed in different places?

Is your bike or mower stuck below tons of household objects discarded?

Is it hard for you to get your car in the garage? If you answered yes to all these questions, maybe it is time to organize your garage.

If your garage were better organized, you could easily park your car there. What a terrific thing it will be! Your garage is not just a place where you must park the vehicle; it is a place to be warm and dry in cold weather. That is why your garage was built initially, wasn't it?

Not just a factory, but even a spot to hold your car away?! It might be a matter of taking the following steps to get your garage back to what it once was.

1 Set up your crucial purpose to organize your garage and decide what you want to store in it. Is the garage going to be used as an example to house your car and nothing else?

Maybe you will even store wood in your garage or exercise area? Should it also be an organized storage area for cars, lawmakers, gardening equipment, parties, billiards, or a man's cave?

You need to mention the forms in which you want to use your garage and the items that are best stored there. When this information is available, start figuring out the different spaces in your garage and how you want to see every room used.

2 Make another list of the things or resources that you need to achieve your objective. You can find it appropriate to buy some racks or containers, maybe a bike rack or two, and place these things on your list.

Make sure you think of any additional equipment that your garage may need to coordinate. There is nothing worse than the completion of all the machinery, but no instruments.

3 Set some time to start the sorting process and categorize the products you have. Rather than hold the job off, you can start the project by setting a specific time and date.

Suppose you are incredibly fortunate if you can room on your entrance to sort out your belongings. The trick here is to clean your garage of all things and sort them out thoroughly.

4 Remove everything from your garage will first allow you to see what you have and what you will no longer need. The proper handling of an old solvent or paint cans, car batteries, and other potentially hazardous wastes is an important consideration. If you are out of the garage, give it a clean sweep. To begin with and to be able to start working properly, you should first have a clean floor.

Consider the space you have when you move everything out of the garage. Using all available vertical room is an excellent way to maximize the number of things that you can store.

Decks and walls can provide excellent storage spaces for objects that can be either packed or suspended. By utilizing hanging bin systems, hanging bike racks, and even floating rack systems, the storage space can be maximized.

5 Categorize the things and remember how much they are used for a moment. Return per category to the garage as much as you need access to it. For example, make sure the children's toys are placed in an easy position to reach.

When it comes to the little things that we still think we collect like knives, tape, screws, and all the odd bits, place them into systematic area like tippers, numbered vases, etc.

6 Establish what you want your garage to use and what kind of things you want to keep. For example, would you like to use it just to park your car?

7 Can your garage double as a workshop or a gym? Or is it appropriate for items like yard tools, bikes, scooters, and some other sports equipment to counter as a storage area? Do you need a place to store your decorations throughout the season?

8 Make a list of items to store, and your garage is very critical. Use the data to classify which garage component is used and what kinds of items are stored in the different garage area.

Make sure you mention any extra supplies, instruments, or equipment, so if you need to purchase shelves, armchairs, hooks, or bins, for example. Make sure you remember which resources you will need to install.

9 Create a timetable if you want to work on the garage and complete the work; the precise date will help keep you organized and avoid it for another time. Take plenty of time to start arranging as well as organizing items into groups in the garage.

10 Use containers to categorize and isolate the different items in your garage. After sorting all this, you can see what you have and how much you have. You will find things that are broken, out of date, or that you do not like. Select all the things outside your garage so you can have them washed, swept, and even decorated when it is empty if you would like to.

Note the unused space when the garage is empty and try to decide if you have enough storage for all your property. Walls and ceilings are useful resources that can be used for shelves, cabinets, organizing networks, cabinet systems, bin systems, and other hanging storage aids. Ensure your parking space is kept in mind if you intend to park your car in your garage.

11 Hold identical items together when putting the items back in the garage. Place all your decorations in the same area, for example. In a designated garage area, bring all your tools and equipment together. The use of labels on containers, cabinets, and racks allows you to remember where the products go once, they are done.

You can park your car in the garage following a few easy steps and get the screwdriver or hammer if you need it. You will know what is in your garage and would like to go there without disheartening because you cannot find what you are searching for. The bonus is the feeling of satisfaction you can experience once the work is complete, and your garage is back.

If you cannot fit your car in a garage, it can cause several issues. First off, let's take it on, cars are not cheap, and having to buy another one is a little embarrassing, not to mention costly due to the fact that you are not able to fit yours in the garage.

Secondly, if you can't get your car into your garage because of the storm, you and everything in your car will suffer as a result of fire, cold, wind, rain, snow, sleet, ice, and other natural catastrophes while your storm sits nicely and comfortably in your garage. It just does not sound fair.

Life is not always fair, I know, but at least in your garage, you should be able to place your car. Let us learn how to arrange your garage and find a way to do that.

I was in my garages, some of them were so packed that you couldn't turn around without overcoming anything, some of them were empty (ok, it was a house just built), and then my dad's garage. He has an impressive garage.

First, it is enormous, and then there is the way everything has got a spot. His garage is so organized that it is a wonder. Did he do it all day? Naturally, he did not even have a garage for a long time, but he arranged it once he designed it.

You do not have to have much storage to have a garage. Your first question should be: what is my garage for? (No, this is not a — gee, what kind of question is this toothbrush for?). Do you want to put cars (or boats) in your garage when I say this, I mean?

Will it function as a workshop?

Do you need outdoor facilities (washing machines, rakes, shovels, etc.)? After you (yes, you use the intent as a verb-if you want a room, you decide what to do with your room), you start the "Steps to Organization" in order to learn how to organize.

The measures towards the organization are evident. Imagine putting a puzzle together. First, what do you do? (Well, you open the box first, but I think we have gone beyond that part.) So, what is the next step?

You start by sorting the pieces depending on the type of person you are. The pieces with right edges go into a pile, and the pieces are back into the bottom of the box without the right edges. Therefore, our first move is:

Step 1 — SORTING

After you have finished sorting your pieces, we will move to stage two. So, what is next to creating a puzzle? Are we working it out and then walking away? Should we first bring together the core (i.e., bits without a straight edge)? No, first, we build our pieces boundary. Stage two is:

Step 2 – A BORDER HOUSE

The frontier has now been established, but we have not finished yet. If you have left the puzzle with only one border, you will never enjoy its elegance. The same applies to the organization. It is nice to create a boundary, but now you must use it. How are you using a border?

 (I am glad I asked you, but I am sure you would have asked if you were here.) We are using a puzzle boundary to warn us about the puzzle.

The border tells us the scale of the final product. It helps us figure out where the inner sections should be and allows us to see the light at the end of the tunnel. (I went from puzzles to trains and I am going to go back soon. It is a mixed metaphor, but I digress.)

Step 3 — Focus IN THE PAYS

It makes sense when you think about a puzzle; after all, you just sit there and wait for the stack of non-straight-facing pieces. How does the company work?

Do you remember how we sorted in stage one? That is our missing parts, so filling the parts means you are putting away things.

So, what is the last movie, then?

Take a minute to think about it-what do you do when you are done with a puzzle? Do you leave it where you have built it?

Do you take something apart so that you can do it again?

Are you moving on because that is moving to become an art piece for you to hang on the wall? We are not, no, yes, for our comparison (i.e., relating the design of a puzzle to learning how to arrange a cloakroom). No, we just do not leave where it is – it just adds to the storm.

STEP 4 — THE FINAL STEP — KEEP IT ORGANIZED (I forgot about step 3, so we can add it here — fanfare, fireworks, and laser light show, just for fun).

Let us look at an example now that we have climbed together on the " Organization steps."

Note: if you only have a limited time to work on your organizational project, then continue going through the steps.

Stage 1: Classification

Since the garage can become a dumping site, it can take quite a while. If you live in a neighborhood or near the main road and want it to be more comfortable, just open your garage door Saturday morning, warm spring, and put a garage sign in your front yard.

If you open it, you are going to come, yard dealers. As you sort, random people will enter your garage and give you money for your mess. This is the moment when you determine if anything should be preserved. If you want to keep something, you could something like this: "I am so sorry, I don't sell it" and guide it to the stack of items you have agreed to split. You might not be the right choice if you live in Minnesota and it is midwinter.

Return to sorting, start with piling – you will need to open a door or move a car (once your car is found) to sort the room. It would be best if you had at least a garbage pile, a donated pile or yard sale pile, a garage pile, and a storage pile but not in the garage.

("keep it, but it's not in the garage pile now, but it's going to have to leave sooner or later")

Be vigilant with this last pile, as the interior of your home will not be littered with, merely to clean your garage out. When you have your simple stacks, look again at the stacks of your two. Look at every object and decide if you need it or not.

If you stick to items from another user, return the items. (If they are the ones who have abandoned them, let them know how to arrange and the average person on the website told them to come over and get their things or they're out on their yard sale.)

Throw away the garbage, sell or donate the pile of "get it out of my house," put the rest away, and then move onto stage two.

Stage 2: House a Boundary

The first thing to think about is how much space you have while arranging a garage. This may seem like a simple query, but do not restrict yourself to the floor space when thinking about space. Garages are perfect for using floor space, wall space, and even ceiling space.

The second thing that should be worried about is PEGBOARD!

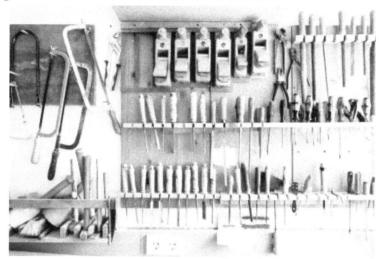

Pegboard is a marvelous thing, and it just looks fantastic in a shed. Most panels are either brown or white (usually one color on both sides). The workers at your local home improvement store will provide installation tips. I recently discovered that they have galvanized steel mats, which look nice.

They have an entire organizing structure to use for the metal panel. What matters is your garage look. The explanation of why it is so large is because it is so customizable.

Below, you can see some ways to adapt your panel.

Advanced hooks

Screwdriver hooks can carry screwdrivers, pins, scissors, and almost anything slim enough to fit into the hole, but they have some sort of top to keep them out.

There are also simple hooks. Simple hooks are long hooks that are directly connected to the wall. Simple hooks can be used for anything from hanging power cords, garden pads, or with a hole in it. I place two of them next to each other and use these hooks to keep our shop broom together.

The selection packages are perfect whenever you need a variety of storage products and are usually cheaper. Some goods have jars that contain nuts, washing machines, or some other small objects.

Baskets and Bins:

Wire baskets are perfect for carrying more massive objects (i.e., things that do not fall through the holes). They are available in different shapes as well as sizes. Accessory boxes are great for larger or smaller objects-they may accommodate small items, and they have sturdy foundations.

Small bins have space for equipment and smaller hardware and items, such as nails, screws, nuts, and bolts.

You should start looking at arranging some of the larger objects after you have possession of tools and other little things. You may pick either a garden tool manager that is on the floor or the organizers of a strip garden tool that is attached to the wall, whether you have more floor space or more wall space.

Consider the different choices while keeping your garage layout in mind and pick what works best for you. There are so many ways to build your garage, but not all of them work for all, as there are garages of all shapes as well as sizes. Continue to create the frontier for your garage; look to the walls when you run out of space on the concrete. If you run out of space on the walls, determine if you need it all and if it is in the basement, then look to the ceiling.

They have some lovely ceiling storage items. There are elevators to heat bicycles on your rods, and you can fit the roof above your garage door; there are so many things cool out there, or you can build your own (just make sure you know what you're doing so that it doesn't collapse on you).

My dad installed wooden racks in his garage and then screwed the jar clothes on the underside of those racks. He uses jars for storing nails, screws as well as all kinds of small items. This is a perfect place to store small articles (the jars are visible), and you can also recycle items you already have.

Stage 3: Piece filling

The frontier is the challenging part. After that, start putting things away. Again, when you position each object, make sure you decide if you need it. You might have to tweak here and there, but as you move on, you will be able to do that.

Stage 4: The final move-Hold it

Do not forget the final movie, which is all significant. Keep your systems running – you must reconsider your system in case you notice that your garage is being humiliated in a short period. If the boundary is not clear enough for everyone to pursue, you will fight uphill. Learning how to plan should not be too difficult; if this is the case, something is not right.

If you can arrange your garage and form your ship, you can bring your car inside. Imagine having a place especially built to park your car! It is safe against the heat, an environment where you can get in and out of your car and stay dry when it is either sunny or cold.

Are these not the reasons why the garage was first built? Not storage, but a garage for your car?! Here are some ways to help you get your garage back and finally be able to take advantage of it again.

Second, evaluate the principal function or intention of the garage and what things you want to store in it. Is the garage built to protect and store your car and nothing else?

Can your garage be a workshop or a fitness center as well?

Will you need to store a wide variety of gardening equipment, family bikes, and several outdoor toys?

From the very start, it is essential to determine everything you want to use your garage for and all things you want to house – it is highly advised to list them first. Use the list and then determine how to use each part of the garage best and store your various items for both quick and practical access.

Identify any additional equipment or storage materials that you may need. For example, you must buy some impressive beams, plastic storage bins, bike racks, tool managers, etc. Any resources you must build these things -do not forget that they must be saved later!

It is important to sort as well as arrange and allow yourself enough time to do so properly. Label your calendar day and time, and do not put it off until the day comes. You must clear your garage completely using the boxes or parts of your driveway to sort and arrange things as you carry them out.

You would probably be shocked by how many things you have and quickly find things to be disposed of or recycled. When your garage is clean, give it a thorough sweep – it may be the only time you will see the whole floor!

Now you can start planning your garage, schedule the amount of room you have, and how it could be used carefully. If you can store more than it seems, explore the use of garage eaves and walls.

These often-forgotten spaces are a perfect way to increase storage quickly. To use all the areas your garage provides; you will need additional shelving or-organized structural grids or vertical storage systems.

Remember to think about how much you place an object in the garage and who can use it. Even though you have more space to reach the tear-washing machine, the children will surely not appreciate their bikes hanging from the ceiling.

Choosing the right room also helps to arrange objects up until the job is completed. You can sort small things in your storage drawer, or if you want your unique storage system, you can cut jars, crooks, and outs for your supplies, nails, or screws.

Not only will you have a place to park your car again, but you will also find everything you are looking for whenever you need to without shifting the accumulated storm by following these guidelines. You will still be remembered the wonderful day you spent cleaning your garage when you enter your garage.

Below you can find a collection of ideas that you can utilize to organize your garage.

Workbench

If you do not spend time arranging your workbench, your garage will never be completely organized. The following qualities should be a strong workbench.

• Solid construction with at least one wide drawer which is conveniently positioned.

This drawer can be used not only for storage but also for dropping your tools when being in a hurry. Throwing tools haphazardly into this drawing might not be ideal, but it is better than leaving them lying around the house in various places and not finding them if you want to.

In case you use the central drawer as temporary storage, I would recommend that you organize this drawer at least once a week by using the tools you threw into it and place it where it belongs.

• Pegboard back for tools and other items to be used.

A pegboard back helps you to buy individual organizers hanging on the pegboard. These organizers can be small containers for noodles, bolts, screws, nails, etc. More organizers may also be hung on pegboards with larger equipment.

• Shelving

Garage shelving is available in various styles as well as sizes. The following are some thoughts about how to install your garage shelving.

• Cabinets built on the wall.

Shelving is mainly used to remove objects from the floor and arrange them. Wall-mounted cabinets not only bring organization into your garage but also allow the locking of hazardous substances.

• Tables for metal containers

Metal storage units are typically independent wall-mounted storage units. Since they are stand-alone units, they can be moved in your garage from one location to another one.

• Hook and Pegboard device

A pegboard and a hook system should be mounted in each garage. Pegboards and hooks give you versatility, from small tools to shovels, rakes, and some other equipment. Pegboards can be placed on any open wall to maximize the amount of room available otherwise.

- Full cabinets

These cupboards can be either free of charge or placed on the wall—full-length closets for rakes, shovels, weed eaters, etc. In case your tools are put in full-length wardrobes, they are not left where you can walk through them.

- Ceiling Storage

Unfortunately, the ceiling turns out to be a waste of room in most garages. The space between the top of your car and the ceiling is suitable for storage and should be used.

A garage ceiling may be used to store several tools and articles, including boxes, lawn, and equipment for landscape design, and other articles and tools not used regularly. There are various ceiling regiments available from your local hardware store, or you can make your ceiling regiments if you are handy to create.

One means of readily accessible garage ceiling storage is the usage of a pulley storage system. You will never have to carry a load of boxes or objects again with a pulley storage system. Pulley systems save you from continuously climbing up and down a ladder so that the device enhances protection. A pulley mechanism is designed to lift and lower the storage shelf to achieve easy access.

As you can see, when it comes to keep an organized garage, there are many choices. It is essential to keep your garage organized periodically in the habit of setting time aside. If you keep your garage tidy, your productivity will increase when you finish your homework.

CHAPTER 18

USE CASES TO ORGANIZE YOUR CLEANING SUPPLIES

Many of us live a hectic life today, so when we find a few hours to clean our homes, we want to have the supplies ready to flow.

You might take the time to track down the cleanser or sprint to the furniture and polish shop to redirect your attention. Makes sure you spend an hour preparing and storing your cleaning supplies before time, so there will be no delays when you are ready to start your job.

To begin with, find a storage place for the larger equipment. This might be a large utility wardrobe or storage space stored in the washroom, cellar, or workshop. A turning handle or a snap-lock allows the cabinet to open.

Even with the cover of a curtain, you can keep the dust mop, broom as well as wet mop, a bucket, sponges, brushes, and some other instruments there. If you do not have a fridge, you can always hold the things in a laundry room corner or a hall closet together. Make sure the environment is safe, clean, and free of moisture.

For cleaning items such as cleaners, polishes, and soap, use a wooden, vinyl, or plastic box. Make sure you find a protected environment in which animals and children are unable to encounter and exploit certain things.

You need to use more than one crate to include your entire stock. In fact, on each floor of the house, you may carry a crate of required cleaning supplies since cleaning requirements can differ.

For example, if the main bathrooms are on the second floor, the cupboard for this level contains bath cleaners, sponges, and, in case your water is difficult, maybe a little rust treatment. Nevertheless, you may want to maintain more potent scrubbing agents and dusters in the basement.

Organize the cleaning supplies inside the boxes, closets, and cupboards as you wish to use them, preferably with the tallest in the back and the shorter in the front. Make sure all bottle caps are securely closed.

Remove leaked droplets or powder until the next time you put away your supplies. Place the sponges or cloths used aside for washing to get them fit for next use. You will often want to scrub the broom, mop, dustpan, and some other appliances to keep them smooth and germ-free.

If supplies are sold for cleaning, store them in your favorites and store them in clean cases or on the shelf at home. This helps you to stop paying high dollars when all you need is running out and shopping in a rush. However, if a product has an expiration date, make sure to use it before this date arrives.

When you are about to start cleaning, do not wait to search for your supplies. It is annoying to pick up a cleaner can for the sink, only to find out that it is empty or like it. Plan, arrange, and save time for your supplies.

CHAPTER 19

ORGANIZING YOUR HOUSE WITH PLASTIC STORAGE BOXES

Would you like to keep your home tidy and clutter-free? All you must do is purchase plastic boxes, which will provide you with a spacious container where you can position your goods to be accessed conveniently later.

In your home, it can be a tedious job to arrange your items and some other things, especially if you have bad memories of searching far and wide to find items that are secure and cannot find them when you need them. You will get rid of this when you start using plastic storage boxes, and you are in a position to handle your things so that you can easily access it if you need it.

Using the plastic storage boxes features, you can easily fit your workspace, closets, and storage areas. Since the storage boxes are transparent and have clothes, you can protect your things properly. The plastic storage boxes are made in several sizes, shapes, styles as well as lids.

If you want to store important papers, you can buy boxes with lockable lids. If you want to use them for your clothing, however, it is quite helpful if you buy plastic boxes of clothing that can be opened or shut without any effort.

It is essential that you first sort out all the clothing and accessories you want to keep for a while before deciding to use the plastic storage boxes for your closet section. You can categorize the products according to their features or the season you need them the most.

You can then start putting things within the boxes after classifying them in your wardrobe. If you use transparent plastic boxes, see what you have placed inside them, it would be easier to scan for something if you place labels on every box.

If you want large objects to be packed, make sure you have large plastic storage bins so that the things do not appear or sprout in a plastic container. Bear in mind that you should bear the boxes that hold the items you often use in a position to reach.

Plastic storage boxes may be bought either from department stores or hardware stores. Or it might be even easier to search the websites that sell these bags in a wide range of labels, shapes, and sizes at lower prices than they are available.

Closets and wardrobes often tend to be smaller than average. Most of us have more and more things over time that we do not want to get rid of. Perhaps it is a picture, or because we hope there is always a possibility in the future to use it again.

Yet, let us face it: most of the clothing, magazines, or anything else we do not frequently use sit behind our drawers, and we neglect even to have them. That is the reason why the plastic boxes are a perfect way to keep items organized and, if necessary, to make them easier to locate.

It is not about making so many unnecessary things with storage issues. Perhaps, you need just a way to arrange your things and give your proper treasure storage.

Therefore, your favorite products will be protected from many harmful influences, and your home can be kept as smooth as possible. The durable materials used for these boxes give a lasting place for any type of item and a lightweight feature, making it even more desirable.

Remember that lifting the material is always not the easiest thing, so it is sometimes nice to use a lightweight material to choose the right event.

The price is another storage box benefit. It is a cheap yet convenient investment that positively makes your life easier. Therefore, storage boxes have become more and more popular. From the standard clear to the edgy colorful, various models must be chosen. There are many different sizes as well as types.

There are square racks, circular or rectangular, partitioned, and even tray sets. The wisest thing is to keep your things in plastic boxes. Use it to store food, clothes and papers, manicure supplies, make-up, or children's toys.

In any case, the boxes can be handy if you need a quick and easy way of organizing and keeping things safe. It is an excellent way to avoid wet weather, damage terminals, and provide the required space.

CHAPTER 20
WEEKEND PLANNING FOR ORGANIZING YOUR GARAGE

T he garages can be a breeze for items that were not allocated to a house or that you want to put away afterwards and then get distracted with something else and

forget about. Several people are using the garage to store it and never used it to

house their cars.

If you're short and need more stock it's great, but if you're not organized, you can eventually purchase duplicates because you can't find it or just waste a lot of time trying to find the product you're searching for.

Project Plan

The first thing to do is prepare a bit. A garage will normally take a weekend to clear and organize depending on the scale, the number of things you have, and the number of team members. Your team can be either friends or relatives. Engage the entire family. I bet everybody has got a couple of their things in your family.

In case you are alone, ask some friends to support and reciprocate with their garage or cellar organization project. Plan a weekend that is available on your calendars and the calendars of your team member. If it rains, you might want to pick another date as a backup weekend.

Schedule it in the morning to give enough time to complete the day's expected measures. You should sort and purge on the first day, and then allocate homes and container on the next day. Make sure you prepare for all days in breaks as well as lunch. When you build your schedule, let all team members know the plan and review it before you begin.

Day 1 -Sort & Purge

Remove everything from the garage and the group together like objects. You are using entry, patio, or lawn areas for each group. You can play this game to make it fun for them. See how many toys you can find in 15 minutes or how many sports equipment pieces can be found in 10 minutes.

One category could be things in the house that have never gone past the garage. If all things are sorted, purge would be the next step. Delete all broken things or things you like, use, or do not like anymore.

Before you upload something to a site, suggest either recycling or donating. The goal is to reduce the number of 'keepers' to balance the storage space available. Bring the things in the house in and place them in their allocated spaces. You must place the guards back in their garage categories for overnight safe keeping.

Day 2-Delegate Spaces

Look at your empty garage and the room you have at your disposal. Space is available in all types as well as sizes. Shelf units, tanks such as plastic bins, empty trash cans, pots or baskets, freestanding tables, integrated shelves, and storage plates in the garage are all considered to be a good choice. Use your hands first, in the garage, and then in your home.

Only extra purchase storage after all available possibilities at home have been exhausted. Make sure the bins as well as spaces are measured to ensure that the storage object fits in space. Develop zones and their respective objects for each operation.

These areas will probably be the categories you decided when you sorted on day 1. Some usual areas include tools and equipment for paddling, sports equipment, vehicle care, equipment, plant food and insecticides. Bear in mind the following tips as you arrange your things in their positions.

When storing things against garage walls, make sure that you have enough space to open car doors.

I am using big plastic waste cans to store garden sleeves.

To hang small tools in the garage or shed, use a plugboard. Draw a contour around each tool so no mistake can be made on where to place it back.

Store the fuels in a shed or on a covered area away from the house on the concrete.

Store hazardous chemicals on an eye shelf on the front of the label to minimize the possibility of spillage from the shelf upwards.

Store garden tools in a sand bucket mixed with some motor oil to keep them clean.

Shop lighter articles and articles seldom seen on higher shelves.

Think vertically if the storage is tight. Bicycle racks and ladders mounted on the garage wall are considered perfect space savers.

CHAPTER 21
HOW TO ORGANIZE YOUR FAMILY TO HELP WITH HOME EDIT

Organizing yourself at home has great benefits, but it can be hard to achieve if you work 40 hours a week or have a family to attend to.

In case you have children, you will know that the amount of mess produced in the house increases exponentially, and it can be a little mission to help them and to keep them tidy after helping.

If you did not teach your kids to clean up when they go from the beginning, starting with their childhood, it would be more challenging but not impossible to do so. Kids in the house mean that you will not progress if you clean up and untidy behind you.

Nothing is as demoralizing as having your work done in short order. The trick would be to use the natural tendency of a child to please, learn and copy what adults do, and learn how to clean as well as maintain their spaces. You would begin by giving them age-specific tasks.

For example, it is quite acceptable for a child aged four to pick up their toys after they have finished playing with them. For older children, they can at least be moved if they are reluctant to help and advise them that they have two choices: either they can sort through their things or you can.

How can this be encouraged?

The best way to ask the kid to pick up his toys would be something like this: "Once you have put away your toys, you can. Encourage them to watch a movie, come to the table to eat, go for a walk to the park, etc."

They also want to do the same when they see you tidying, as listings tend to emulate the older ones around them.

When you say, "do this before you can do that," you also show them and expect them to finish one thing before going onto the next one. This is an excellent habit of developing and growing up with them. When you add, "after you have finished this, you can do that," you also tell them they can do things. This is a much more efficient saying to consider than "you CAN'T DO this until you have done that."

Not only can you teach them healthy dressing habits and complete activities, but you also inspire them to see life from the viewpoint of CAN.

It will be beneficial and will certainly motivate them to move on with their lives.

Using some of these strategies for the practical side of organizing your house:

Demand your family's support if you live with your family. After all, in this case, not all the mess and confusion will be yours.

Tell them that, as soon as the house is cleaned as well as organized, you will all enjoy living there as soon as possible, and whenever visitors come by, instead of feeling humiliated by the state, you will enjoy visiting them at home.

Getting your home organized can make it a lot easier to find everything you are looking for, and it is going to be a place for everything to put away. Part of the problem with a bogged down-home is that there are so many things that, most of the time, they do not have a place to be located.

When you have inspected everything and found a place for everything, which might include things you have held, storage, and a heap of items, you are going to keep your home nice and tidy. If you were successful in arranging your things, it would not be too difficult to keep the house that way.

The advantage of cleaning with a team effort is that you can organize yourself at home much quicker, and everyone can feel happier once the job is done. The positive side effects of your children often do not want to rush out their excellent work, and they will always hold others accountable for keeping it safe.

So, how can you get started?

The first thing you need to do is to have a strategy. Decide how and when you want to do this.

First, get all the supplies and equipment you need to clean and organize your land.

After you have sorted everything out, you have a pile of anything you do not need or want anymore. You can give it away or sell it in case it is still in an excellent working state, and you are pleased to know that you are recycling valuable resources instead of only throwing things away.

Knowing that you also support others is a beautiful feeling and promotes caring for and sharing with your children.

Organizing at home has some significant spin-offs and reduces your stress.

If you have done that, it is easy enough to hold it. It is significant. Why was all this hard work wasted to plan such a big project again later?

To keep your house safe and tidy, do a little bit until it is a routine each day. Replace the old habit of putting it off by forming a new habit today before tomorrow.

You can also help your family make it a routine so they can learn how to organize themselves. This can then become part of daily life, but it will certainly make a difference for your stress-free life!

CHAPTER 22

FOLLOWING THE LATEST HOME ORGANIZING

TRENDS

C oncerning organizing patterns at home, they tend to be evolving alongside home decorating patterns. However, if you can grasp the key patterns in all

household trends, it is much easier to adopt new trends.

All house-organizing trends are focused on productivity, secret storage as well as convenience. Here is an overview of what these three fundamental issues mean:

Effectiveness

Space management is a key component of performance. There are a lot of excellent organizational resources available, but they are just not right for your room. Efficient space management means that it is the best possible choice in each space.

For example, in case you have a small living room, the best option is probably the massive wrap around couch and large screen TV. Instead, it would be much easier to have a fairer size TV and a love chair, two tables, and a tiny table too.

The concept of space efficiency is particularly important in times of economic slowdown, as the notion of "wasting" becomes much more frowned on than in times of economic boom.

Storage Secret

There are a vast number of flexible items that can be used for storing random things. Decorative boxes/containers are one of the most famous examples. These containers are designed to be supplementary decorations and accessories in a room but can also be doubled as a storage tool. Several pieces of furniture are another example of this.

There are beds underneath that have drawers; there are tools that open and carry magazines or some other items. To fall into this group, something must be decorative and still have the additional value of secret storage.

Convenience

There are many different areas of fashion that will shed comfort as well as convenience to increase visual appeal. For example, if you organize your home office, would you like to store all your pens in the room?

Of course, you do not want them to be on top of your desk in a desk drawer or a cafe. This also ensures that you keep items in order of priority. If you use items regularly, then items that are used less frequently should not be protected.

This issue usually arises in kitchen cupboards. You may have a bigger product like a blender, but you keep it in the back, so it fits in smoothly in the corner. Although it fits in the corner, it is not considered to be the best position.

Home organization patterns will still evolve as interior design patterns shift. In all these shifts, however, three basic laws will still be implemented. They must use productivity, secret storage as well as comfort to be genuinely successful for organizations.

Keeping Track of Your Important Documents

How is your home organized? Could you find it if you want your birth certificate in a hurry? How about your auto insurance policy or the medical history of your child?

What several people do not know is that it involves understanding where all the important things are. Not only is it so safe and secure, but it is also a place where items can be kept and easily found.

It is a critical part of your company to have a fireproof safe for all your valuable records and papers. A list of all your valuables and images is important as well. You might also want to make a video of each room.

Wouldn't it be helpful to have an inventory list and a snapshot of your family heirlooms if your home were robbed when you were out for dinner?

It is, of course, a fact that people who have pictures of their valuables are more likely to survive and come back. If your records are lost or are shoved somewhere in a shoebox, you might never be able to get your jewelry back.

You would have unexpectedly another emergency on your hands if you did have an emergency, and a neighbor came to sit with your child and didn't realize they were allergic to peanuts and feeding him a sandwich of peanut butter. Anyone needs to know where the medical records of your child are stored.

If you had a burn, will the insurance company take your word when you said you lost a $2,000 HD tv, 52 inches? Perhaps not! Record the transaction and tape it to the sales receipt together with a photograph.

Even though no one wants to think of a beloved death, it will be good and less painful for the remaining spouse or family member to know where important paperwork such as life insurance policy lie. This tip should be at the top of your list as you arrange your important documents.

Clutter tends to bring needless stress to mind and well-being of an individual. Trying to put your finances in order is an endeavor you can only accomplish, but many items can help you in the organization of your garage or cupboards. Check out some of the great things.

Space bags are the ultimate commodity in the organization of closets. They are so flexible that you will wonder how you ever worked without them after you have tried it. They can be used for coordinating and traveling at home.

When you camp and cruise, space bags come in handy. You wonder, then, what are they? Space bags are insulated storage bags, airtight, waterproof, and reusable. These bags can store clothing, sheets, towels as well as silverware.

They minimize the room used in your closet to 4 times the amount of space already used. This is a great tip. Here is a great tip. Keep your bits of silver in a space bag to avoid tarnishing.

If your wardrobe is out of place, space bags would be helpful, but you would also want to look at a shoe storage system. It will not be advised to place shoes on a space bag.

Storage racks and plastic shoe boxes are available to store and shape your shoes. Shoe bags are also available, but they must not be confused with the spice bag. When trying to organize your closets, a shoe storage device is certainly a smart idea.

If you want to clean up your garage, garage organizer products are a great way to do this. There are wall organizers, shelves, racks, and overhead brackets that can be purchased to help you understand your garage. If your garage organizer system is in operation, your equipment, car supplies, garden equipment, and sports facilities can be stored in an organized way.

Now that you have some organizational product ideas, your life does not seem more structured. Use space bags in your home for every room or closet. A shoe storage system in your wardrobe and a garage organizer system for your garage will provide you with some stress relief. Once all your rooms have been in order, you would have a disorderly free mind to begin to get other things right.

The other day I saw a TV commercial for one of those goods that promise to give you a little bottle with hours of energy. The man in the shopping cart pulled himself out of the house, complained about how long it took to prepare a cup of coffee, bathed the bottle, and went to work with joy.

That is how I feel right now in the morning, not because I drink anything, but because my wardrobe has been organized, and I am dressed up in a short period of time. I am no longer disappointed by the clothes I am searching for since I cannot find it.

Closet, a crucial domestic organization tip, is making this a breeze.

I began my journey in the closet by determining which groups to put in each cloth sweaters, tops, trousers, and so on. Then, briefly, I could see what I had and how many of them I still need.

Then I began to clear up the items I had stopped wearing long ago (or cannot fit in anymore). I had been bringing a couple of fun t-shirts from Ireland years ago, but I could not wear them for several years.

If you wear a lot of seasonal clothing or sports clothing at certain times of the year, think about getting them out of your wardrobe and sticking them in plastic bins. I like the clear, hard lid plastic bins you will find at either Target or Wal-Mart.

They are just a few bucks, and you can see what them at a glance is inside. Consider storing them in the attic or the garage before the right season. The hard cloths seal the containers well and keep bugs or varmints out. They perform much better than carton boxes!

At many times per year, you might start changing your clothes by exchanging summer clothes bins with the winter clothes in the wardrobe, and vice versa. This method makes it much easier to find what you are searching for in the closet.

The next thing I did was sort the clothes on the hanging rods in the closet into "working" clothes and casual clothes. My closet has the door on the right and goes deep to the left, where it is more difficult to see and enter.

So, I place the workwear on the right side of the closet to easily get to them while I work. In the morning before work, I am quite often in a rush and have less time to fool myself in search of things. When I get home from work, I have more time to dig deeper into the wardrobe, so that arrangement is more suitable.

I have put some medium-sized hooks for smaller objects that appear in the corner to be shoved or fall to the floor. This is a perfect way to bring all the belts together and bind them together. Consider also obtaining a collection of hooks from the top of the closet door. Just be careful not to place so much on the hooks that it becomes difficult to close the closet door.

You can use many other little tricks, but you get the basic idea. It does not have to cost you a lot of money because you can find shelving and hooks at your nearby dollar shop.

Why panic each morning when you can make your life a little bit easier?

CHAPTER 23

HOME ORGANIZATION TIPS TO KEEP YOUR HOUSE NEAT AND TIDY

O rganizing your home is a process that can be both difficult and frustrating. When presented in its entirety, it can also be considered difficult to achieve.

However, if you plan to approach this issue step by step, it can be considered

much simpler than imagined, making things more effective and helping you spend your time in a productive manner.

Before something more can happen and you decide to take care of it yourself, here are some ideas for a home organization that might support you. Like any critical project, the first thing you need to do is to draft a proposal, as it will act as your handbook in case you leave.

Take time to split your strategy carefully into various tasks so that you can concentrate in the right direction, and to simplify things so much when attempting to achieve your goals for such a big project as organizing your house.

Concentrate on one room first or on a particular section of that room before moving on for some days or weeks to get things in order. It would be beneficial if you first wanted to focus on the most challenging areas, such as the kitchen or the living room, all of which see a lot of action every single day.

If you want to start from scratch, eliminate everything in that place. It will allow you to determine how you want things to look, where furniture or appliances, and many other considerations are considered suitable.

If you have objects or products that you may think are either useless or unusable, delete them without hesitation.

If you have clothing or furniture you do not need any more, donations can be made, or you can even sell a garage to help you afford new materials for your home. For things not donated, you can keep them in storage by using cardboard boxes or containers that you can easily maintain in the attic or cellar of your home.

You can then arrange anything you want if it makes it easy to achieve and comfortable to live. Organize your clothes according to what you wear. It takes some common sense when you look at it to find out how you want the whole house to be organized, but it cannot work out according to those circumstances.

It will take a while before you feel comfortable about how things are organized. When the rearrangement has been completed, you can make sure that you know how to manage it by monitoring where certain things belong and preserving other things.

It can be an arduous job to find the best way to clean and organize your house. House cleaning with these few tips can be made simple. If you do not clean and organize your house regularly, it can become filthy as well as unorganized, and you can never find something. House cleaning can be fast and straightforward if you try to divide all tasks into smaller parts one by one.

Cleaning and preparation with time-saving tips:

When you're about to have dinner, fill your sink with soapy and hot water; all you need to do is place the vaulting and other utensils in the sink when you're finished, and they will take some soap until you clean them.

Before you do your laundry, it is very tiring to figure it out. If you have many smaller baskets, you can sort them accordingly and fill them, then the next one. Cleaning rooms can be tedious, but it helps when you buy large items such as toys and clothes and pass on to the smaller ones.

Cleaning and organizing ideas for cleaning:

If you do not clean regularly, your kitchen disposal might become very smelly. A quarter of a lemon (it helps to cut the smell) is a fast and straightforward way of doing that; about half a cup of salt and three ice cubes will do the magic.

Then run your disposal for a few minutes with hot water, and your disposal is as right as new. When washing, always make sure that your sponges are thoroughly rinsed to avoid mildew accumulation and prevent smells. After you clean them, zap them for a few minutes into the microwave to kill the bacteria.

Cleaning and arranging quick organizational tips: the first cause for chaos is that people take things out and fail to put them back.

The job of cleaning rapidly is to place a shoe organizer in your wardrobe so that when you have more time, you can put these things in it and deal with them. Hold just books in them for bookcases. Do not store anything and everything, or it is just going to become another trash spot.

Tips for efficient organization and cleaning:

A wise selection of furniture; check for items that can double as storage. Keep things in large label cases for children's rooms, you know where it is, and the child learns to sort its toys and other items as well.

CHAPTER 24

DE-CLUTTERING AND ORGANIZING YOUR HOME WITH SIMPLE SECRETS

I n this chapter, I've listed simple secrets for decluttering and organizing your home with ease

1. Reduce what comes in your house

Remember this basic rule to reduce what comes in your house:

For example, I look at what I have before I go shopping when I buy new clothes, but I am not ending up with four white t-shirts. When I come home with a couple of jeans, two blazers, and a jumper from my shopping trip, I look at what is going out the door now.

That may be the old articles I am replacing or just other clothes; otherwise, my wardrobe will soon become a catastrophe. The same applies to furniture (without filling a new home or having no furniture), and other household objects such as candlesticks, servings, etc.

2. Keep it out of the kitchen!

One thing I train my clients to do is to keep their homes intact by refusing to put any things in the house first. Junk mail, leaflets, car trash, and unwanted objects are only a few things to avoid. To stop it, I sift my mail and flyers close to the garage where recycling and waste are stored. Then I can get rid of what we do not need immediately. I do the same for our car garbage.

The minute we get out of the car, at the gas station, or home, whether we get fast food or take-home church newsletters, the garbage is gone! You may say no to friends, relatives, or neighbors who load you with garbage. If you do not like the item that they send to you, but they demand you have it, throw it in, or find someone else that wants it.

This may sound cruel, but it is the push of other people in our lives that we take what we do not want. Email operates the same thing. The first thing I do is highlight all junk and press delete whenever I open my account.

I can concentrate on the relevant messages once the trash is out of the way. It also frees me from heaps of spam messages using my storage room. Think about what things like this you should remove.

3. Don't hold things you do not want!!

This may sound bizarre, but you would be shocked by how many customers I worked with; they genuinely think things are hideous or do not suit any room at home! Do not keep on old furniture or sackcloth's that you got because you were given by a loved one.

Only send the products to someone you know who wants and who needs them. If this is not an option, offer it or sell it on eBay and make some money while you are there! In this area, too, it is good to be proactive.

I almost stuck with many old furniture; my grandmother was preparing to move to a nursing home. I just had to say, "I'd like to, but I just can't. It prevented a great deal of lifting, transport, and storing unnecessary things to appease it.

4. Do not store things of other people in your house!

When we are talking about "storing" objects, it is never a good idea to store products for acquaintances, family, or neighbors. They are sometimes adamant about going back, but they often do not. It keeps you in contact with unnecessary things from someone else. If you are in this position right now, call these people and remind them that you are doing a 'spring cleaning.'

5. Have a measurable de-cluttering goal!

You must have goals for anything you want in life. It is no different to organize and rid yourself of clutters in your home. I know the piles can be overwhelming, but when you have a goal, you will not only feel in control, but when you finish it, you will definitely get guidance and a sense of satisfaction, for example, if you want to clean your cellar or a closet.

6. Launch Small

Most of my clients called me to support them because they felt overwhelmed by disorder, mainly because they did not know where or how to start. It did not have to be complicated or tired. If the room is too big for a day, spend 1 hour per day on any part of the room, like every dresser cupboard, on Day 1, and what's underneath the bed

7. The secrets of Lisa step by step to organize any room.

You do not have to be the Rocket Scientist. First, pick one bedroom at a time like the spare / guest room. Make four piles in that room. One pile is for garbage, another stack is for things you don't want, and the third pile is for objects that belong in the house like oven mitts or CDs, and the fourth one is for things you don't want but would like to donate.

I know that the time you spend organizing your home will give you such an incredible sense of achievement, enrich your mind and make you want to deal not just with other areas of your home, but keep them that way!

CHAPTER 25
QUICK TIPS TO ORGANIZE MESSY AREAS OF YOUR HOUSE

No matter how hard you try, some places in your home still look messy as well as confusing. Not only is your house dirty, but you also spend more time trying

to clean things up and waste time searching for products whenever you need

them.

Furthermore, studies show that an orderly house encourages calmness and stress reduction. Try these storage tips to help reduce the chaos, save you time, and provide yourself with inner peace.

Kitchen Cupboards

What do the cupboards inside your kitchen look like? Does it look like a puzzle in which each piece suits perfectly? Or does it look like an open-ended puzzle box with all the pieces jumbling together? If your wardrobes are not arranged to the degree you want, try this strategy might help you find a solution:

Use trays (or tension rods like the adjustable rods to hang coffee rings) to store trays and cookie sheets lined vertically for flat products such as platters, trays, and cookie sheets. You can access what you want faster, and you can stack your bowls, pots, pans, and some other things with more space.

Install a sliding shelf organizer in your office to make your pots and cups available. Sliding drawers make it easy to locate things that seem to be misplaced and overlooked in the back of the cabinet. The installation of a lid organizer inside the door allows you room to store all your wandering garments.

Medicine Cabinet

Real estate comes at a premium in medical cabinets. Each time you open the door, avoid products falling out by removing unnecessary uncertainty. Only keep things in your drugstore several times a day, such as a toothbrush, toothpaste, and face wash.

Return your medicines to a different space. Removing them does not only generate more storage; it also protects your medicinal products since they are not ideal for the steamy and humid bathroom. Divide your other standard bathroom products into bins or baskets under your sink using purpose (hair, makeup, etc.).

Closet Linen

When changing your bedsheets, it is a struggle to find all the different parts that fit. Avoid pain by storing your sheets in packages of pillows. Fold together all sheets and all but one packet and bring the folded linen into the remainder of the bottle to make a clean packet.

On the middle and lower shelves, maintain regular towels, sheets, and other linen and store unused items like holiday tables, towels, and extra beds on the rear or tougher shelves. Once a year, go through your linen closet, give away everything you do not need, or throw out anything either ripped or worn out.

Sink Room under Your Kitchen

Often the space under your kitchen sink can look like the legendary junk drawer. Remove cleaning as well as spongy items with the Lazy Susan. A Lazy Susan is an ideal way to store all your cleaning products; it is just a spin to get to the window cleaner or all-purpose spray.

If you have ample space for a Lazy Susan, mount a heavy-duty tension rod and hang spray bottles from the rod. Install hooks (one with a sticky backrest does not leave marks) at the cabinet doors for a position where dish towels can be hung—using low-cost plastic containers to category group cleaning products-glass cleaners, stain removers, carpet cleaners, etc.

CHAPTER 26
ORGANIZE YOUR HOME ONCE AND FOR ALL

Home organizing is simple, and, for several people, a constant activity. For many people, making time to keep their homes organized and tidy is a top priority.

For some people, however, the home organization is not at the top of the list until the challenge is too wide to be overlooked. Besides, it can be easy to organize, but it is much harder to maintain a tidy, uncompromising house.

Home edit is a two-stage operation. Step one is the organization of your house, and step two keeps this business. That means, of course, that stage two is an ongoing operation, that you are not doing it once and done.

Holding the hard work of your home organization would be a permanent part of your life. The good news is that if you have a maintenance schedule, managing it would be more straightforward.

If you have not spent much time with your home in the past, it can be an awful chore to both clean and organize your house. The bigger your house, and the larger your family, the more organized it seems. Chaos can take over in the long term. It can seem like organizing is unlikely at that point. However, by taking those steps, you will certainly organize your home once and for all.

Embrace your space

To accept your space, you must accept that maybe you do not have room for all the belongings in your home now. It is more complicated than it seems! Nevertheless, this is a big step in organizing your house because you would end up with more clutter if you do not acknowledge the space limitations.

Eliminate the rubbish

It can be fun to eliminate the clutter of your home, but several people find it difficult to think they may have to get rid of some of their favorite things. The trick is to hold what you cannot do without and tell the rest. Give away things, donate to a charity shop, or shop in the barn, cellar, or garage for things you are not sure about until you know whether you need them or not.

Find a home for all things

After your de-clutter, you will be left with the things you love and what you love, and now is the time to find the right home for each piece. In practical artifacts, the safest way is to store things in the space where they are used the most. For instance, gardening tools should not be stored inside, and any personal grooming should be in the bathroom or the bedroom.

When you need homes for products, think about investing in storage containers and space savers. These kinds of things, from spice racks to bathroom managers to shoe trees and storage bins, will help you to organize a home in an instant.

Delegate Responsibility

If your children's rooms are in a messy condition and keeping their rooms tidy is an ongoing challenge, bring it on them to clean up their living spaces. Inform your children that it will be their duty from now on to keep their bedrooms clean (or not clean).

As a parent, you can provide instructions, a plan, and a timetable to clean your rooms, but the job itself must be done entirely. Make sure they understand that you will not dig your room for dirty laundry or wipe up spills.

This technique will not work for all families. Individual parents find that it not only eliminates the burden of cleaning those rooms but eliminates a source of tension in the relationship between parent and child the responsibility for the cleanliness and organization of their child's bedroom on the children themselves.

Maintenance

When the initial task of home organization is complete, it is time to advance to the next challenge: keeping your house well-ordered as well as uncluttered. This can be challenging even if you are single and living in a reasonably small apartment; but, if you have children in the house, a consistent home organization can be more challenging.

The critical thing to remember is to establish and conform to a schedule. You do not have to do it all in a single day. If you continue to do your routine, you should be able to keep your house in order daily.

Set aside sometime every day for repairs or pick one space to focus every day. So, you will not have to do it at once, and you can spend a small amount of time keeping your home organized.

The organization is not an add-on to what you are doing today; it replaces destructive behaviors with excellent as well as efficient actions. So, the organization takes less time than disorganization.

Second, you can quickly start implementing the decluttering plan; you'll get the support you need to change your thinking, change your actions, and build a home of which you are proud of.

Start now with these five simple techniques to reduce the number of non-essential things (clogging) you carry to your home.

1. Take a list at the store.

Market analysts say that two-thirds of the purchases we make are items that we did not plan to buy at the grocery store. For instance: The scent from the bakery will make you feel hungry, and you buy more food while you are hungry. Solution-Shop when you have had to eat and just buy things on your list.

Children's toys are intentionally placed on the shelves in the lower store, so your children can pick items and cart them. Solution: Schedule food shopping when you can go alone and only buy things on your list; save time and avoid a fuss with kids.

Supermarkets are organized to enable you to shop more. The dairy section (essential for most families), for example, is in the back of the shop. This layout is designed to pull you deep into the shop to buy more along the way. Solution-Take the shortest route to the milk sector and only purchase products from your list.

The longer you are on the market, the more items you are going to purchase.

Solution - Do do not go all aisles down. Shop in aisles only, buy only things mentioned on your list, and get in and out as efficiently as possible. Purchasing products that are not listed also leads to duplicates and uncertainty. Furthermore, it is not your best use (time and money).

2.Tell family or friends who want to give you their downs.

Say "No" in case people around you sell things that they do not need or have space for, ask yourself the following questions:

Do you love this item?

Do you have a comfortable and attractive room for the item?

Can you use the item enough to carry it home?

If all three questions can be answered, "Yes," honestly, embrace the article. Otherwise, it is yet another piece of the hurricane.

3.Step clear of spur-of-the-moment shopping.

Impulse purchasing usually means that you have the chance to understand where you can hold an item and how much you will use it. Think about it twice:

Bring home souvenirs for the holidays.

Register for magazines and books or DVD clubs.

Buying on QVC and eBay late night

Mall shopping or niche shopping

These are just material things, so you probably do not need any of them. Save your money for debt service, create a solid financial base, and do good worldwide.

4.Reduce your receipt of junk mail.

Did you know that you can receive up to 500 pounds of junk mail within one year?

Do not let your room or time read these things anymore:

If you ever get a junk mail after following this technique, throw it directly into either your wastebasket or recycling bin.

5.Inform gift donors if they would like to send a gift certificate, gift card, or a charitable donation in your name. You have probably never used gifts, and you will never use the room in your house, but when you do not want to offend the gift-giving, you hold on to them.

If your thoughts reflect that feeling, it is time to reframe your thoughts. Holding gifts that you would never use is not an opportunity. It is a burden. You are robbing your room.

Give donations to a charitable organization that you do not need and let anyone else enjoy them.

The 21-day practice of these techniques will surely allow you to establish an essential habit of decay. At the same time, you will find that implementing this idea into your life will save you both time and money and give you the confidence to deal with the next steps.

CHAPTER 27

QUESTIONS TO ASK YOURSELF BEFORE YOU ORGANIZE YOUR HOUSE

O ne of the hardest things to do at times is to keep your house tidy. The reason it needs to be organized is that a messy house causes so much chaos and makes you waste time while looking for things. An ordered house runs smoothly.

There are many available ways you can arrange your home.

You should ask five essential questions to organize your house quickly.

Tip No.1-Have you have been using this item in the last six months? -If you intend on decluttering your things, you need to be ruthless in your approach.

Any space you must plan must be scrutinized thoroughly. Each object in each room must be scrutinized thoroughly. Ask yourself basic questions like when you last used them if you have not used something for more than six months, so it must be trashed. You can delete this thing from your rubbish portfolio.

2-Will you need it in the future?

There are some exceptions to the 6-month rule or Tip No.1. If the object is something you use in the future, it does not necessarily have to be trashed. Some examples are those seasonal objects appropriate seasons, such as warm clothes or umbrellas, etc.

Each item that is not used more than six months should then be validated for the other condition if the item is needed at some point in the future.

3-Do you have time to accumulate the item?

Some people are accustomed to collect books, compact records, or music collections. They compile these sets, but they seldom use them. The book racks are filled with books, but not even a page. Next time you intend to buy something, make sure you do it twice. Otherwise, do not continue with the purchase.

4-Is it difficult in the future to substitute the item?

Until you start to organize your items, will it be complicated or straightforward in the future to replace this item? If its value increases with time and becomes something like ancient, then the safest way would be to keep it. Some good examples are jewelry or paintings; the older it gets more costly.

5 – Do you spend too much time organizing?

Some people take so long to plan things. They are used to twisting things. They fear starting their job, or they fear even choosing to unravel things. The only answer to this? Do not take the time to decide.

The implementation of these five tips, or at least consideration when you decide to arrange your home, will change your attitude drastically in cleaning up your disorder inside your home.

To arrange your house

You have fallen into the houses of toys, dumb garbage, rotting leaves, loose socks, weekly sandwiches, and even worse. You probably have also visited houses where there was not just a crumb or speck of dust.

Trendy, some houses are embarrassing while others are spotless. The trick is down-to-earth diligence as well as organization.

If your company continually fails or panics, it may be time for them to organize your house. The first and most important thing to do to coordinate is to stop. It is painful, complicated, but it is over. Move around a space and take all the shelves and dressers down.

Create three stacks, one to hold, one to waste, and another one to give away. If your living room with your pile is considerably bigger than the other two stacks, you are not doing an excellent job of leaving. A cozy home can be a place where everything is clean and plain, not overcrowded with distractions.

Some measures use the items you thought we would show. You may send it to the Salvation Army, Goodwill, or other organizations to implement the regulations. Or, if you are very excited about quitting, you can have a garage sale and raise more money. What you are trying to do with the garbage is rejoice when you legally get it lowered—making it worthwhile. You certainly deserve it.

The next thing you need to do is locate some organizational devices. Things like tables, files, and tubes can be used for holding the things that you are trying to preserve. Gather your things into groups that make it easy to find.

Use various organizational resources to discover the completed job. When you reach this point, bed, closet, or drawer should not be there; you fear opening.

When you plan your own house, you can take pictures of your home protection system. Do you need to pitch it and get another one, or will it still work? If you do not have one by anyway, you may want to add one. If you see that the house looks fantastic, it needs to be this way.

CONCLUSION

We get so distracted at times that we neglect the organization of our homes.

We are living in chaos and sleeping in disarray. This can cause a lot of tension and household tribulations.

While some people are lovely with this arrangement, a lot of people are sick as well as exhausted. You can use many resources and tips to organize your house. All you must do is know what they are, and you are going to be tidy and organized.

To start organizing your home, the first step is to decide how much mess you must go through. While keeping this in mind, you will get an idea of how you arrange your house. At this point, you must note that you cannot do everything in a short period of time, but careful preparation will certainly help speed the process.

Since cleaning seems to be a lot of work, you can make your favorite music more enjoyable and quicker. The next step consists of having three boxes or big bags and marks them with the following names:

"KEEP," "DONATE," and "TRASH" This would be an essential tool so you can bring each object out of the floor, the racks, corners and beds and sofas into one of the containers.

Then list all the rooms in the house and the items that should be inside. The list of things for each room should be the essential elements only. This makes it easier to remove waste and repair. Then you must choose a room to start with. When you have selected one, you will determine more easily what you will do.

For example, first, you choose your bedroom. You must determine what kind of furniture and furnishings to hold, and you must unplug your wardrobe. Place the products in your box or bag. Go the same way through all the rooms in your space.

At this point, you must have weeded all your belongings already. If you do not use an object much, save it more frequently from the way you use it. In general, if you have not used or worn an object for one year, either donate or throw it away.

Take the "TRASH" labeled bags or boxes and put them in the right waste can or employ someone to take them away. Place all the "DONATE" bags in the garage if you cannot give them away immediately. You must, therefore, ensure that they are taken to the donation centers as soon as possible. When everything is done, organize everything left so you can find it quickly.

You can also add a few more decorations to embellish your house. You should also tidy up your house and organize it as much as possible. You should buy a calendar and write to your newly arranged space at some periods. Color-code your calendar so that you can choose meetings times, deadlines, and appointments in a quick manner.

Housekeeping or cleaning your house is a word that differs from person to person in a personal context. Many of them have no proper sense of storage, and anywhere they collect their things, but adequate knowledge of the arrangement and location of your house can change the decor and clean the room. House cleaning be challenging work, but with a few tips, it no longer must be like that.

You should plan properly to organize your home. You must first take care of your household that is chaotic as well as unorganized. You then must determine where to place and install the suitable furnishings in a room. Bear in mind that a room should not be wasted with incorrect furnishings and showcases; use the space for useful items instead.

Cleaning a bedroom needs little effort. However, you must keep it tidy and hygienic and arrange your home. Bed sheets should be adjusted regularly; the curtains should be either cleaned by a vacuum cleaner or washed. Furniture and objects must be kept free of dust. The cobwebs should be cleaned by a sponge.

Generally, a kitchen needs a lot of cleaning since it is a busy space. To properly organize your house, particularly the kitchen, you will need a maximum of two days. On the first day, the refrigerator, the oven, and the stove can be washed. The next day the roof, walls, and kitchen cabinets can be washed.

Cleaning a bathroom may be a hectic work, but it can seem to him/her less laborious if you know any tips on House Cleaning. Next, you should go to the bath and shower, lavatory, and a rag or a sponge in other places. It should be almost a regular task, as it is always used.

During the house, you should not neglect the teapots that adorn your floor, as it can be a refuge for many clouds of dust and bacteria. It should be periodically washed with a vacuum cleaner and cleaned up the spills as soon as possible.

With all this in mind, we must note that living in a clean home and having an organized lifestyle will, without any doubt, make your everyday routine more productive and peaceful while at home.

Best Wishes

Lightning Source UK Ltd.
Milton Keynes UK
UKHW050024030522
402289UK00017B/385

9 781801 219778